IN AT THE DEEP END

IN AT THE DEEP END

Paul Heiney

Foreword by Chris Serle

METHUEN

By arrangement with the British Broadcasting Corporation

To Agy, Bollio and Tim – the
ones who never complained

First published in Great Britain 1986
by Methuen London Ltd
11 New Fetter Lane, London EC4P 4EE
Copyright © 1986 Paul Heiney
Printed in Great Britain

British Library Cataloguing in Publication Data

Heiney, Paul
  In at the deep end.
  1. Great Britain – Occupations
  I. Title
  331.7'02'0924   HF5382

ISBN 0-413-42380-8

Contents

Illustrations

1a At the Waterside Inn with Michel Roux
1b With teammate Mark, agonising over the *agneaux*
2a Early training days – John Parker at his most worried
2b The Duke of Edinburgh points out the intricacies of dressage
3a 'First' – after presentation and dressage
3b Bollio and Agy plunge bravely through the water hazard
4a Terry Scott warns me: 'You say, I'll go and sweep the roads, but let me out of this agony'
4b Marti Caine gives Ada the northern touch
5a Last-minute exhortations from Jimmy Perry
5b Make-up man Bert Broe creates the 'Ada look'
5c Ada . . . 'I'm not the woman I appear to be'
6a A friendly lick from Tim
6b One man, his dog and a flock of stroppy sheep
7 A nerve-wracking moment for Jilly Cooper, just before the first cut
8a Kessler, trying to 'think like a mugger, a man who would barbecue his own granny'
8b Michael Caine gasps at my bravura performance

These photographs are reproduced by kind permission of the BBC (1a, 1b, 4a, 4b, 5a, 5b, 5c, 6a, 6b, 7, 8a, 8b), the Swan Lane Studio (2a), the Press Association (2b) and the Norwich Union Insurance Group (3a, 3b).

Acknowledgements

Ventures such as these are not possible without an enormous amount of goodwill and encouragement from all who take part, and I would like to thank all those who have dedicated hours of their time and no small amount of their patience to teaching me their skills.

I must also take this opportunity to thank those whose names do not appear, but without whom none of these adventures would have been possible: the researchers. Fran Landesman for unearthing the romantic writers, Peter Grimsdale for discovering John Parker and his horses, and Jo Clough for not only bringing to heel Tim the sheepdog but for gathering together the finest chefs in Britain and not once allowing these volatile men to boil over.

For turning miles of film into fifty gripping minutes of television, credit must go to an unbeatable team of popular-documentary-makers: Patricia Houlihan, John Bird, Ruth Jackson and above all Nick Handel – described by Michael Caine as 'the tall geezer from the BBC'. With Nick I have shared some of the highest moments and a few of the lowest too. Although he has been on the safer side of the camera, I know that he has suffered as much as I have, if not more.

Foreword

When you apply for a job they ask you if you have any experience. Paul Heiney and I have spent years trying for a succession of jobs from which, if we admit any experience at all, we are instantly disqualified. From a position of utter inadequacy we've been thrown by our bosses at the BBC right in up to our necks. We've tried, God we've tried. But under the all-seeing stare of the cameras we have more or less consistently logged a personal achievement score of zilch.

It doesn't seem long since he and I were summoned to the BBC for a meeting with a senior executive. We had decided to leave our jobs on the consumer programme *That's Life*, which propelled us from obscurity to ratings of 17 million in three years. We were famous and jobless. 'You've still got a few months left on your contracts. We can't have you sitting around here doing nothing. What do you intend to do next?'

Mumbling something about looking for worthwhile projects, we had to admit the offers hadn't exactly been pouring in. I was seriously thinking about going back to my old job as a television producer.

'How would you like to try a new programme in which you are seen having a go at other people's jobs? We thought of calling it *Jobs for the Boys*.'

With the rapier decisiveness we knew he liked we said, 'Er, could you tell us a bit more about what's involved?'

'It's like the series we've been doing called *Big Time* in which members of the public fulfil their wildest Walter Mitty dreams and become wrestlers, cooks, pop singers and so on. The difference in your case is that you would be reporters and job-tryers at the same time. An American journalist, George Plimpton, did something like it ten years ago on television over there and it seemed to go quite well. What do you reckon? Think about it carefully and let us know.'

We thought carefully for about a second and said, 'We'll do it.' Paul and I were In at the Deep End.

Since then, with the help of some of the most gifted producer-directors in television, we have been making series after series of highly successful documentary films whose most memorable moments are our failure to achieve anything approaching the standards our mentors expect of us. Luckily ego or vanity are not at issue. If we did turn out to be any good, how would it make the experts look? What is far more important about these brief fifty-minute glimpses behind the scenes is the insight we get into what makes top professionals and enthusiasts tick.

All makers of documentary films about people have to invent their own ways of helping their subjects appear as natural as possible on the screen. When a jaded film crew, who have seen it all before, have filled your room with cameras, lights and sound equipment and then get down to the serious business of drinking your tea in readiness for the first shot of the day, you don't always feel at your most expansive. And when the reporter launches into his carefully researched questions before you're even sure if the camera is running, it's a miracle that anyone can manage more than a prolonged clearing of the throat.

In at the Deep End is different. For one thing we usually interview people while they are doing what they do best, their job. They are usually at the top of their professions so they tend to want to impart some of their enthusiasm for what they do. And on our side we are asking questions from a particularly committed point of view. We are not just prompting responses for the sake of 'getting some good quotes'. We are trying to find out as much as possible about the job so that we can genuinely have a go at doing it. The resulting answers come out a cut above the level of a prepared press statement. We always find our contributors eager not only to tell us how to do the job but to offer

unexpected wrinkles and tricks of the trade to encourage
us do it as well as they do. They always want us to
succeed. The fact that they are giving us the benefit of
twenty years' experience guarantees that in just three or
four months we will never be a threat.

While Paul has been diving in at his various deep ends,
including, now, writing the book you're about to read, I
have been trying my hand at an equal number of occupations. In case it's not absolutely clear to you we are in
alternate films. I'm in the ones he's not in, and vice versa.
While he's been learning to drive horses, tell jokes dressed
up as a woman, be a film actor, and so on (see book), I've
been finding out what it takes to be a butler, a rally driver,
a Latin-American ballroom dancer, a snooker player, an
auctioneer, an opera singer, a yacht skipper in the Fastnet
Race, a Fleet Street photographer and a race course bookie.

The question we are invariably asked is, 'Which is your
favourite?' It's a bit like asking a parent of nine children
the same question, but undoubtedly the one which caused
the most personal grief was learning to dance the Paso
Doble for a ballroom-dancing competition at the Hammer-
smith Palais. Having to dress up in a one-piece stretch-
fabric cat-suit when one's natural dancing ability is on
a level with a one-legged half-drunk orang-utan is not
something I would readily repeat. It didn't help when we
enlisted the coaching skills of one of the country's top
dancers, Wayne Sleep, and the kindest thing he could
bring himself to say was, 'It's hard to know what to say.
There's so much wrong. We must remember there are
boys *and* girls and we *must* make the difference.' My only
consolation during a disheartening few months was that
most of the men who would watch the film would know
just how I felt. We certainly discovered just how much
selfless and antisocial dedication goes into that glittering
world where, for just three or four minutes, a shorthand
typist from Penge can step out on to a dance floor in a
glittery frock and be a princess.

To pick a favourite is impossible. To say that we have
had the opportunity of meeting some of the most gifted

and dedicated people in the world and asking them a question almost unique on film, 'I want to do what you do. Can you show me how you do it?', and that we've found the answers challenging, rewarding and above all entertaining, is understating it by a mile.

Chris Serle

Preface

Some years ago, as Chris Serle has explained, we were asked to report on a series of professions by joining them and working to the standard set by our tutors. Our tuition and our progress were filmed at every stage, and the price we had to pay for any glory that might fall on our shoulders at the end was the humiliation heaped upon us as we trod warily through the various tasks.

Each programme told a gripping story, but it was never the complete story, simply because the programmes lasted a brief fifty minutes on television when Chris and I might have struggled on for months out of sight of the cameras.

During those months, relationships were forged with our mentors; friendships were formed, as were a few enmities. Many of them could not be reflected in the brief span of the programmes, but to me they were the most important part of making those films. That is why I have written this book. It is about how *my* life has been changed and how, many months after the completion of the films, the joys and the miseries can still live on. Some of my early adventures I have been able to recount with the benefit of hindsight, others I have recorded as I struggled on.

If you saw the television programmes, then I hope this book will help you to reflect on them from a different angle. If not, do exactly as I was asked to do: plunge in at the deep end. If you learn half as much as I did, I will not have been wasting my time.

Paul Heiney

Anguish
and
Agneaux

Anguish and Agneaux

What is sauce for the goose is sauce for the gander, except at the Waterside Inn at Bray. No such unsubtle assumption would be allowed here in Michel Roux's prize restaurant.

The Waterside Inn is one of the top half dozen restaurants in this country. It has three Michelin stars to its credit, which does not mean that it has any connection with the motor tyre business (although spare tyres are probably one of its by-products) but rather that the inspectors who compile the Michelin guide to hotels and restaurants, a bible-sized red book, consider it to be amongst the best. They hand out stars like the Queen hands out Maundy money – only occasionally and not very many at one go. They also prefer to dish them out to Frenchmen, and no English chef has yet achieved three.

But Michel Roux is used to the burden of Michelin stars. With his brother Albert, he has climbed the gastronomic ladder from his parents' butcher's shop to ownership of a chain of London restaurants (including the three-star Gavroche) and a pinch of consultancies: amongst them, taster of pastry for Marks and Spencer and cuisine adviser to British Airways.

The Waterside Inn is his home (his house is next door) and since 1974, when he bought what was a run-down pub and set about turning it into one of the finest restaurants in Britain, his working life has been devoted to excellence in food. Twelve years on, he is not fully satisfied, although most connoisseurs would say he achieved his goal years ago. His struggle goes on, not only to produce the best food, but to search worldwide for the finest ingredients and to scour the catering colleges and dingy hotel kitchens for talent to do them justice.

And where do I stand on these culinary slopes? Somewhat nervously, I find myself at the peak. Unlike most chefs, I have not had the chance to get a footing on the nursery slopes of washing-up or potato-peeling, but, like a reluctant boy prince, I have had the tall white crown of the chef's hat placed on my head and in a couple of months I am to take the place of Michel Roux, and represent his beloved Waterside Inn, in a cookery contest against three other top restaurants. I have a lot on my plate.

If jobs are best tackled on a full stomach, I am going to be well prepared for this one. For the first and only time in this enterprise, I am on the customer's side of the green baize door tonight; I'm dining out at the Waterside. I have yet to meet Michel Roux, or see the kitchen, so my mind is clear to concentrate on the food. The menu is in French, of course, which makes it difficult when you do not know your *rognons* from your *brochet*, but the waiters are too well trained by Roux to intimidate or patronise a customer. So, after an uneducated browse through the menu, I settle for fish, followed by duck, and reserve my options on the pudding.

I don't have to linger long on the cocktail of champagne and passion-fruit juice before I am invited, not rushed, to the table. It is dusk when I sit down, so the river is no more than a sparkle in the gloom. The colours of chairs and decoration merge under the dimmed lighting to give an air of intense relaxation; stepping into this dining-room is not unlike sinking into a comfortable seat in a theatre. The waiters are like dancers in some well-rehearsed routine, enacting a ballet around you. One boy will sweep in with bread, while from the other side a man will pounce with wine.

There is just time to take in the beauty of the drooping willow tree that has its roots by the window and its branches tickling the Thames ('I bought this place because I loved that tree,' says Roux) before the first course arrives. It is carried proudly, chest high on heavy silver trays which stretch the waiters' arms to their limits. Vegetables decorate the tray – beetroots and turnips carved into the shapes of flowers. The food is hidden and there is a routine to be gone through before you catch sight of it: a dazzling silver dome that covers it has to be removed, with the sort of flourish a magician uses to pull the rabbit out of the hat. If you are sitting opposite a lady then hers will be lifted a fraction of a second before yours. This way, the waiter can extract two gasps of delight from his clients.

Which brings me to the food. This is the most difficult thing to assess and the likely root of all my problems: palate. It's going to be difficult for a lad whose mother was a firm believer in some brown powder called Burdall's Gravy Salt, and who started the cabbage boiling at nine in the morning to be ready for a one o'clock lunch, to get used to the notion of the crisp and scarcely cooked vegetable and the sanctity of the natural juices of food that have to be blended into a sauce – a sauce which is there to complement the food and not simply to provide a pool of slop in which to push your mashed potato. In other words, I am eating (and will eventually be cooking) out of my class.

There is a clash, like the meeting of two cymbals, as the silver dome is removed from my plate. I see pinks, and pale yellows, and white. The pink is *langoustine*, an enormous prawn, the pale yellow is of spaghetti in a sauce and the white is the flesh of small pieces of fish. If you have never eaten food of this standard before, what might you expect? Is the earth going to move, is there going to be a fanfare of trumpets when the first forkful hits your tongue? I raise the first taste of it to my mouth, and smile. You smile because it is a delight, a caress to the tongue. All the flavours are discernible, not submerged in salad cream or Burdall's Gravy Salt.

Or are they? For just a moment I remember the story of the emperor's new clothes. It would be a brave man who stood up here and said that this was no more than a plate full of spaghetti with a few prawns and a lump of left-over cod in a puddle of thin, white gravy, especially when the bill is going to come to fifty quid a head.

While these unworthy thoughts are crossing my mind,

the emperor himself appears: Michel Roux. He is dressed in a starched white chef's uniform but with a few brown splashes down the jacket to show that he is a working chef and no mere restaurant manager. He walks briskly, talks crisply through a heavy French accent and, although his penetrating blue eyes are set on me, his radar is taking in every movement of his waiters. When he is not in the dining-room, he will use his scanning closed-circuit television camera to locate any slackness, and pounce if he spots any. But he's in buoyant mood as we discuss how I can possibly learn to cook to his standard in a matter of months.

'No problem. I shall teach you personally . . .' He pauses, flicking his eyes towards the waiter. 'I have been looking at my watch. You have been waiting thirty seconds longer for your coffee than I would have liked. In my London restaurant that would be unacceptable but here in the country it will do. Just.'

The waiters overhear this and there is a nasty collision as pots of coffee are rushed in from all sides.

It's no use asking questions, since he has an uncanny knack of anticipating them and giving a full answer well before the question has finished. Believing this to be my first and last meal at the Waterside (all my subsequent visits will be confined to the kitchen), we part with a firm French handshake and a beaming confident smile, from Roux anyway. I glimpsed my own face in a passing silver dome, and it just looked puzzled.

On my second visit to the Waterside I did get another meal, and in the dining-room too. But this one was on somewhat different terms. I arrived already dressed in the required blue-and-white check trousers and chef's jacket, with my hat folded under my arm. I was in time for the 'staff meal'.

Roux serves food to chefs and waiters at six in the evening. That way, they have full stomachs when the evening's work begins and can resist all temptations to scrunch petit-fours.

'Oh God! Not duck legs again,' grumbles one chef. Another mutters in French, which I don't understand, but from the look on his face the message is the same. There seems to be a duck-leg surplus. Breasts go on the diners' table; legs are left to be scorned on the staff table. They tasted good to me, but then I hadn't seen the more succulent half of the duck from which they came.

Since half the staff are French, the meal is a more serious affair than if they were a group of Englishmen having their tea. Although no wine is served (only Malvern water) glasses are held by the stem and swirled as if their contents were fine claret. Bread is broken and not cut, coffee is toe-curlingly strong and cheese finishes off every meal. I wouldn't be surprised if they complain about the cheeses too. They're the dog ends from the customers' cheese trolley, but still way ahead of your average bit of supermarket vacuum-packed.

Roux appears and beckons me into the kitchen for a whistle-stop tour.

'This is the . . . [can't understand the French] where the meat is . . . [French again] . . . vegetables are put in the [more French] . . . and we never use any [and more French] . . .'

I nod feebly, hoping for a friendly Englishman to fill in any gaps. It is a beautiful kitchen, as clean and orderly as a laboratory. No accumulated grease in forgotten corners, no corners at all really – just vast surfaces of stainless steel, polished every day. Beneath each work surface are refrigerated cabinets and, forming an island in the centre, a group of stoves, ovens and grills where twenty-gallon pans containing bones in brown liquid bubble perpetually. Smaller pans are coppered on the outside and gleaming. It is clear that those who work here take a pride in it, and it is also clear that each chef has his workplace and Roux doesn't expect him to wander far from it. But at least they can chat to each other, forbidden at some of his less relaxed restaurants.

'So now you know where everything is in the kitchen,' says Roux, telling, not asking, me.

It's halfway through lesson one and I am in tears. The cause? Onions.

'Not onions,' says Roux, 'shallots. We import them from France.' Much of what is eaten at the Waterside started its life on the other side of the Channel. The Brits apparently can't be trusted to raise even a humble cabbage or cauliflower properly, so refrigerated pantechnicons snake their way weekly from the Paris markets, to dump tons of fruit, veg and meat in a walk-in fridge at the back of the car park.

An Irish girl tries to show me the easiest way to peel onions, but she's hardly picked up a knife before Roux's radar has picked up a lack of a metal dish into which the peelings should fall. She is sharply rebuked and moves on to the carrots. Again she picks up the knife and Roux's steely blue eye is on her again.

'Don't peel over the rubbish bin. Peel on to a tray and then into the rubbish bin.' It's one metal dish for the peeled carrot, and another for the peelings – you can tell that chefs here don't do their own washing-up. Yet the poor lad who does always seems to manage a smile, even when he is up to his elbows in greasy water. He is a chubby Frenchman (perhaps Brits can't even be trusted with getting the pans clean), wearing a moustache and a pair of calf-length pink rubber wellington boots. Like everyone in this kitchen he has his own secret recipe; in his case it's for an abrasive mixture involving salt, sugar and vinegar with which he restores the copper pans to a dazzling shine. Although he's the person with the muckiest job and the least to smile about, he cheerily scrubs away, and when he's not there (for he also acts as liveried doorman) a miserable lad takes over and casts a shadow over that end of the kitchen.

I'm going to peel an orange and break it into segments. Roux has told me to. So I pick up the orange and reach for the knife and I'm wrong already. I'd forgotten the metal tray for the peel to fall on to, so I sheepishly make my way across the kitchen to the pan rack next to the washing-up sinks. With an apology for creating yet more superfluous washing-up writ large across my face, I grab an old tin and return to my corner. I start to peel. The Irish girl tells me to peel down, a lad tells me to peel round and round. Roux has disappeared so I let instinct guide me and hold the orange on the chopping-board and slice down.

'Paawl!' I hear the deep throaty Gallic roar behind me. Roux has come back. His penetrating boom reaches, like his gimlet eye, into every recess of his warren of a kitchen and probably into the car-park fridge as well. I'd backed the wrong horse.

'You hold the orange in one hand and peel round and round,' he tells me, and with a turn of his knife he carves an orange as perfectly round as a ping-pong ball. Pity it's going to be broken into pieces, but clearly one must not only strive for a perfect end-product, but entertain nothing less than perfection along the way. What is out of sight is not out of mind, and a segment, even if perfect in itself, would – if carved from a ragged orange – stick in a gourmet's gullet. I find all this difficult to swallow.

Semi-hypnotised by the pointless task of accurately dividing this orange into its pieces, I go into a trance and break out of it only upon a shout from the cooks. As orders, hastily scribbled by waiters, are passed to the head chef, he shouts them out in French through a loudspeaker system. The butchery and pastry sections are around a corner and, without a loudspeaker, orders might take some days in getting there. The chef mumbles in French, and with the unity of Hebrew slaves, the cooks reply with a chorused 'Chef!' You can read a lot from the way they say it. 'Chef' can either be shouted with enthusiasm or spat out. It can be delivered *sotto voce*, as it usually is when the deputy chef is in charge, but when it's Roux it comes out crisply and in unison like the fall of soldiers' feet on the parade ground.

It only stirs me for a moment from my orange-segmenting, and then I am back into my trance.

'What are these bits of orange for, anyway?' I eventually ask.

'Only a garnish, a bit of decoration,' says the girl.

But this, of course, is decoration to the highest standard. I'm not yet in a position to pass judgement on the taste of the food but I promise you that you won't find any better *looking* grub anywhere. Humble lamb chops and vegetables are arranged as carefully as jewels on a ring; they are bit-part players in the great theatrical experience of eating at the Waterside, and at the moment that the silver dome is whisked off them and they meet the customer's eye for the first time, Roux expects a flawless performance from them.

The deputy chef gets a message from the head waiter and picks up the phone. He speaks to Roux, in gabbled French and with a look of concern on his face. The television monitor, which has been blank all night, is switched on, and with an array of remote controls the hidden camera zooms and pans round the restaurant under the direction of the head waiter. It settles on a table where two gentlemen are sitting chatting.

Roux rushes into the kitchen, preceded by a bark at the vegetable chef,

'I want to taste *everything* . . .'

'*Chef!*' is chorused loud and strong like I have never heard it before.

Roux puts on his white hat and takes charge at the stove. As dishes are prepared, they are tasted first by the under-chef, given the nod of approval by the deputy chef, and then often rejected by Roux.

'Too much saarrlt . . .' or 'Not cooked enough!' and a young chef, half-terrified, will start again from scratch.

Roux has taken charge of all the pans now, and is stirring and tasting and adding to them with much waving of hands and arms. With a spoon, he'll taste his sauce and, with the commanding hand-movements of a conductor, food will be placed on plates and sauce poured round it. Round it, you will notice: not *on* it. They say the difference between this style of cuisine and good old-fashioned cooking is that here, the gravy goes on the plate first.

It is a few minutes before I discover what all the fuss

has been about. I put down my knife and macerated orange, which has suffered a little due to my attention having been elsewhere.

'We think it's the Michelin inspectors. The head waiter thought he recognised them,' I am told.

Cunning swines! It's a cold Tuesday night in early February, just the sort of night when a restaurant might be running in a lower gear than usual, and that's the night the Michelin men choose to pay an anonymous visit. Devious they might be, but their importance cannot be under-rated, not to Roux anyway. To hold three Michelin stars is like getting your Oscar. It is a mark of supreme excellence. They can't take Oscars away, but Michelin will whip the stars away if they don't like what they find on their unannounced visits. It is said that one set of inspectors (not Michelin) saw an eminent chef on television being interviewed in his kitchen. Behind him was a catering-sized drum of Bisto. The restaurant and chef were duly demoted.

Roux seems satisfied. He has despatched a perfect beef stew and has kept an eye on a perfect pudding of biscuit filled with fresh raspberries. The kitchen takes on the atmosphere of the lower decks of a frigate after a successful battle has been fought. Roux may put the fear of God into his lads, but they'll go to the ends of the earth to cook for him. He's relaxed now. The steely stare of his eye has gone and he wears an enchanting Gallic smile. You can see why his chefs would die for him.

If you want to know how to make a team of chefs desperately unhappy, I can tell you: you cook lunch for them. This is my first mass-catering experience. I am given fifteen onions to peel, twenty apples and three plastic bags full of a revolting dark-brown slimy snake about five yards long. It turns out to be the French equivalent of black pudding and its appearance is met with a groan by those who loathe it, which is the majority. The staff meals, it must be remembered, are effectively school meals here; there's no choice – you eat them or go hungry. Most of the chefs are young, unmarried and lodge in rooms, some above the restaurant itself. It's like boarding school and I find myself in the position of being the creator of the least-liked of the regular staff lunch dishes.

I spend an hour peeling and slicing onions, another half hour doing the same to the apples and then attack the vast length of the black pudding. There's no secret to cooking the onions, except that of lifting the pans. They are copper and very heavy and the handles get as hot as the pans, so there's a knack to lifting without burning yourself. I have yet to master this. So too with the tossing. Instead of going through a panful of apples and turning each one over, by lifting the end of the pan and bringing it sharply down – at the same time pushing it away from you to catch the apples after they fall – you can flick them all over in one movement. I do manage to flick them all over, but sadly all over the hotplate, where they start to burn and fill the kitchen with the scent of scorched apple pie.

'Look in the oven, see if the black pudding's ready,' shouts a chef. But I'm too dizzy. I know I've only got my mind on three things – a pan of apples, a pan of onions and a tray of hot, oozing black pudding – but I'm already feeling like the circus performer who has to keep his plates spinning.

I have found a good way of testing when food is cooked: you ask one of the lads. He gives the thumbs up and I emulate the Roux artistry by carefully arranging the pudding pieces end to end with a hint of apple just showing beneath a subtle layer of onion.

'Stop mucking around,' shouts one of the lads, who whisks the tray from me and pours it on to a serving dish in a great heap. He then takes a big flat spoon and levels it out, like a man laying concrete. Not many Michelin stars in this.

Having played my big scene I can now step aside while the dish is whisked into the restaurant where the senior staff eat. There's another groan when they remember it's black pudding day. The odd ends of cheese do good business and my first-ever creation is allowed to sit, congeal, and look very sorry for itself.

'Pity you got the black pudding to do,' says one of them, by way of consolation. 'Wednesday tomorrow, we have monkfish on Wednesdays.'

'Bloody sharkmeat *that* tastes like,' said a cross Aussie.

It is time to consider the three other teams of competitors, who come from the Sharrow Bay Hotel in Ullswater, the Manoir aux Quat' Saisons in Oxfordshire and Chez Nico, near Reading. If you have no knowledge of the present gastronomic state of Britain, it is difficult to describe how foodies revere these restaurants. If they were paintings, they would be Leonardos or Turners; people come from miles to see, and to eat. But the seeing is almost as important as the eating. These restaurants set out to make eating a total experience for the eye as well as the palate. Hence the reputation of the famous Sharrow Bay Hotel, where your eye can move from the luxurious menu to the vastness of Ullswater outside the dining-room window. One is eating amidst mountains, and critics have said that the generosity of the portions can make it feel like *eating* mountains, but my childhood led me to believe that it is no crime to have plenty on your plate, and no disgrace to finish it all up.

What a nice couple the two chaps make, the patrons at Sharrow Bay – Francis and Brian. Their relationship has lasted a good thirty years, during which time Sharrow Bay was named Hotel of the Year and Restaurant of the Year in the same year – a unique achievement. Francis is the thin one, the slightly older-looking one, the head chef and a great one for clasping you firmly by the hand or putting a comforting arm around a shoulder. Brian, on the other hand, is round of face, cheery of smile and unstinting in his attempts to satisfy your slightest wish. In fact, he can often pre-empt a wish and a cup of tea need only cross your mind for it to be halfway down the corridor from the kitchen complete with a freshly baked biscuit and an offer of a sandwich. A man could accept a helping too many at

Sharrow Bay, just to see the smile on Francis and Brian's face when their hospitality is accepted.

Although I would not dare say it in front of Michel Roux, what they serve at this hotel is my idea of food. You can have a good slice of a roast, they will not roll their eyes if you ask for Yorkshire pudding, they will press upon you Francis's toffee pudding, made to his own recipe, which melts in the mouth like no pudding I have ever tasted before. And they love to see you enjoying it. Francis will bounce into the dining-room, his chef's jacket rakishly unbuttoned, and urge more food upon you. Not all of it is made up of calorie-bombs, however; some will be light mousses of fish in delicate sauce arranged on the plate *nouvelle*-style. I could get carried away by the Sharrow Bay and sink forever beneath the chintz and the fluffy cushions never to reappear, but I fear the experience of competing with them. They stand in a class of their own. They're a world apart from the creators of fashion food, and I suspect that this contest is more likely to be fought over the slice of kiwi fruit, the emblem of the 'new cooking', than over the most sublime version of roast lamb and gravy.

I had always thought the slice of kiwi fruit was a bit of a joke. One food writer, tired of its appearance on every dish he was served, described it as the 'medallion' worn by *nouvelle cuisine* – the style of cooking which another frustrated writer and eater, describing a particularly thin and watery tomato sauce served under an *hors d'oeuvre*, said looked as though the hostess had cut her wrists while dishing up.

I am surprised to come across a slice of kiwi fruit on my dinner plate at Chez Nico. Nico is an unlikely man to follow any fad. If Sharrow Bay is the most welcoming place you can imagine, Chez Nico is one of the most challenging; you are on your guard from the moment you step through the door of the recently converted rectory set in what Nico calls the 'silicon valley of Reading, Basingstoke and environs'. It's just off the M4 and you follow the signs to the Food Research Institute. Chez Nico is next door.

It's a happy juxtaposition really, for Nico is a one-man

research institute. He is the ultimate processor of food, but instead of emulating his colleagues in the mass-produced food business his efforts are directed entirely at processing everything *but* the goodness out of the food. Take his mushroom consommé for example. It is brown, and quite clear, yet he has instilled into it the perfect flavour of the mushroom. It is as if he has perfected a magic technique for separating food from its flavour and, with a wand, can drop it in wherever he likes. Nico Landenis is striving for two things in life: perfection in food ('My friends say to me, Nico, how can you make it any better?' but I always try) and a Michelin star to add to the two he already has. That would make him the first non-French chef to have three stars to his name and the happiest man on earth. He has a reputation for sharpness with his chefs, and with his customers too. He is said to have let it be known when he thinks his customers might not have ordered what he considers to be an appropriate combination of dishes.

But he's not sharp with me. Quite the reverse. 'I'm worried about you, Paul,' he tells me, fixing me with his dark eyes, 'very often amateurs can win.' I smile, unconvinced. But, he confides, 'You can reach this sort of standard if you avoid the early pitfalls of the cookery schools and catering establishments. You have to find inspiration. My vocation in life is to prepare fantastic food and I will move heaven and earth to do it.'

Having decided early on that much of the modern style of cooking depends for its success as much on the arrangement as on the food, I ask if I'm not better taking art lessons than cookery lessons.

'There's a lot of cowboys in the business,' he lowers his voice, and a hint of an eastern Mediterranean accent filters through. 'I heard a story the other day of someone who devised a new dish. He said he got hold of a breast of duck, he slit it down the middle, stuffed it with lobster, cooked it, made a sauce with mango and paw-paw . . .' his voice rises in incredulity. 'These are the cowboys, these are the charlatans.'

Sounds good to me.

But at least Nico is not a Frenchman. The Gallic turning of the consonants in the back of the throat is beginning to be a little repetitive as I wander amongst the culinary giants. Raymond Blanc, chef and patron at the Manoir aux Quat' Saisons near Oxford, is another of those French chefs who are full of life and enthusiasm. He looks more like an athlete than a chef. No barrel belly on him, he looks as tanned and youthful as Sebastian Coe. As temperaments go, he is reported to have a three-star one to match his cuisine, and reports abound of him flinging himself to the floor during the service of food, weeping in dissatisfaction at his chefs. He seems to have perfected a technique for outwitting the seasons, too, for although it is early April, he manages to serve asparagus and fresh wild mushrooms. 'Do not worry about the competition,' smiles Blanc, 'you English are good at being the losers.'

I mark his team down as one to watch.

There is one clue as to what will be required of me in the competition. The judges have decided that the main course will be shoulder of spring lamb, and I am to cook the main course. The other ingredients will not be revealed until half an hour before the competition starts. There could be anything – we might open the box and find a boar's head. As one chef said to me, 'Don't worry. There's bound to be eggs and flour. You can always make a pancake.' Mmmmm . . . boar's head pancake, with a slice of kiwi fruit . . .

It is clear that cooking has got little to do with gas rings and saucepans. Once you have got that far, you are on the home stretch. It is like painting a front door. Slapping on the paint is the easy bit, but hours of tedious preparation determine the end-product. So it is with cooking.

Roux has taken over my tuition and not the slightest inaccuracy in my slicing will escape him. It's no use slicing an onion unevenly and putting the ragged bits at the bottom of the pile; he'll turn it over with his fingers and you will be sent back to the chopping board. So I learn to slice with precision, both shallots and mushrooms, and then I learn to 'sweat off' . There are two reasons to sweat in a kitchen. One is to extract the natural juices and flavours, usually from a vegetable, and it is done by gently cooking with the smallest amount of butter until, in the case of onions, they become transparent. The other reason to sweat is because of the intense heat of the stove, and in this case it is the poor chef who loses his natural juices. Standing by some of these hotplates is like standing in front of an open furnace. The heat sears your skin and you can feel your eye-balls going crispy. So I develop a strange technique for stirring which makes use of the longest-handled spoon I can find and I operate at arms' length.

I didn't expect sculpture to enter into the game, but I now find myself not only peeling potatoes but carving them and hollowing out the centres so they can be stuffed with thinly sliced leek and carrot. This makes for the most labour-intensive form of vegetable cookery you can imagine: twenty minutes to finely chop the leek and carrot. (*julienne*, as we chefs say) and another ten minutes to carve the spud. Thirty minutes to prepare, one and a half mouthfuls to consume – try giving it to a hungry lorry-driver and he'd tell you where you and your three stars got off. But this is the Roux way of doing it and, as one frustrated chef at the Waterside told me, 'There's only one bloody way, and that's *his* bloody way!'

Of course, slowness with the chopping knife has nothing to do with a lack of manual dexterity on my part; it's just a wish to hang on to all my finger-ends as the knife, honed to a surgical precision, inches closer with every slice of a wobbly onion. Roux, on the other hand, has been concentrating on more important things: the shoulders of lamb. The obvious thing to do with a shoulder of lamb, in his opinion anyway, is to get the bones out of it, stuff it and roast it. Sounds very English, pub-lunch cuisine almost, but stuffing and rolling is too obvious for Roux, so he devises an approach which will be original, yet attain-able even with the most meagre selection of ingredients in the surprise box.

To work, it needs two shoulders of lamb, an egg, onions,

mushrooms, cream, parsley and a remarkable amount of patience on my part, for this is where my fledgling career takes a new turn: I am required to become a butcher.

Now, I'm not squeamish about meat but I have never envied butchers when I've seen them at the back of the shop, working over a barrel of blood and offal with both hands inserted deep into a chicken. I suppose I must be thankful that at least the shoulder has been separated from the lamb for me. I set to work, reluctantly.

It is very often on the butcher's block that a restaurant's profit is made or lost. Flesh left on bones can add up, over a time, into pounds if not tons of good meat thrown to the pigs. Better to carve the bones clean and let the paying pigs get a chance at it. I find boning very anatomical, not unlike the biology classes at school where we would slice through an earthworm in search of some Darwinian truth. You start with the blade bone and carve the meat from it with smooth strokes of the knife. You then score round the edges and, with a primitive display of brute force, you drag the bone away from the flesh. I once had a dislocated shoulder, and I had always wondered how they put it back. Presumably this in reverse. Perhaps that's why I wince as I tug and twist at the remaining bones, slice through tendons, and bend bones in their sockets till they grate against each other.

After twenty minutes (five if you're good) you end up with meat, fat and skin, and all that remains is to separate the three elements to end up with pure lamb flesh which shall be the basis of the dish I expect to cook. The skinning could drive a man crazy. You might as well ask him to sort out the pebbles on Brighton beach or count the blades of grass on the Wembley pitch. Just when you think you have located the last bit of fat or gristle and sliced it off, you turn over your piece of meat to find acres of flab still dangling and you hack away at that. Then a piece will turn up, somehow, in the centre of the chunk of meat. And you dare not miss it, for Roux will be round to inspect. At my first attempt it takes me three hours to bone and carve the lamb: the whole competition only lasts two and three-quarter hours.

Roux is not here on the big day. None of the patrons turn up for the competition except for Brian and Francis from Sharrow Bay, who have dressed their team of chefs in blue blazers. They look like an Olympic squad about to go on parade. My team is more of a shambling affair, but we do seem to have brought more equipment than most. Chris and Mark are my team-mates. Their job will be to cook the first course and the pudding, and for this they have arrived with everything from the rolling pin to the ice-cream-making machine. It will be sandwiches only at the Waterside today.

We set out our stall in the swish new kitchens of the Westminster Catering College, where the contest is being held. We've forgotten half the food-processor, but Raymond Blanc's lot have forgotten their aprons so we do a swap. At eight-thirty sharp, the boxes are brought out. I dive for the one with the bloodstains – the box with the lamb shoulders. Some lamb! twice the size of anything I'd seen before.

'Lamb? That's last year's mutton,' grumbles a chef.

The list is generous. All I need for my dish is there: eggs, cream and all the vegetables. There's also a lobster and a salmon for which I can think of no use, so I leave that to Chris and Mark. There's also a bottle of Grand Marnier, dark rum and a pint of white wine. I note them well.

At nine sharp, I take out my butcher's boning knife. By nine-fifteen I have all three bones out of the first shoulder and by nine-thirty have the bones out of the other. It is very relaxed, so far. I cannot see how I could fail, with two hours still to go, and I check the bottom of the box to see if tea-bags were on the list. A cup would slip down a treat. By ten-fifteen I am worried; this lamb was the Bunter of the flock and removing its fat is a lengthy process. Especially when I see that Sharrow Bay and Blanc's team aren't bothering at all and look set fair to come up with a good old roast joint. Nico's lot look in trouble – one lad has already got a bandaged thumb. I check again just to make sure the tea-bags weren't hiding under the five pineapples. My mates are getting up a head of steam. Lobster flesh has been made into a mousse and parcelled within the sliced salmon, Chris is making biscuits and glancing from the mangoes to the ice-cream maker. He is hatching a plot.

Quarter to eleven and it's only an hour before my dish is due to be presented but at least I've got all the meat away from the fat and cut into cubes. I've found a new technique: you throw away the bits you can't be bothered with. This reduces the work considerably and if there's not enough on the customer's plate at the end of the day, you can always call it *nouvelle cuisine* and double the price.

With the meat trimmings I make what my mother would have called rissoles. The competition rules say the dish must serve eight people, and with only two shoulders of lamb that's pushing it a bit. So Roux taught me what is basically an old housewives' trick: to mince the meat, bind it with an egg (and cream if you're well off or in a competition) flavour with parsley and Bob's your rissole. Except we call it 'a forcemeat' and serve it in the shape of quenelles. Quenelles are small sausage shapes. Forgive me, but I can only describe them as what a naughty schoolboy might draw if he wished to represent horse-droppings.

Hell! I haven't even started the vegetables. But Chris and Mark are on top of that one. I'm left with the shallots to chop to transparent thinness. Then the mushrooms too. It's easy to tell when mushrooms are chopped: you stop when you think you've done it, and then you chop them twice as finely as that.

I sweat off the shallots, then the mushrooms and sprinkle with salt. This gives you a *duxelle* which goes into the forcemeat with a little left over to stuff into some excavated mushrooms. Scooping the middles out of mushrooms while the clock is ticking away is not the most relaxing of pursuits.

'For God's sake get the mushrooms fried,' shouts Chris.

Temperatures are rising. The only thing keeping its cool is the ice-cream machine which, under Chris's command, is churning out mango sorbet.

I add the *duxelle* to the forcemeat, stir in the egg and a little cream and, with two teaspoons, turn blobs of it into smaller but more shapely blobs. Bullet-shaped.

'Get 'em in the pan!' orders Mark and they're in the frying pan and into the oven before I can say 'what the hell do I do next?'

If I were on my own I would be hours behind by now. Nothing has prepared me for working at this speed, or taught me how to have three hands working at once. My lunch would be more of a high-tea, if Chris and Mark hadn't got the sculpted spuds and stuffed courgettes into a pan, while I was still rummaging through my rissole ingredients.

But I'm back on time now. All I have to do is cook the lamb, which takes a matter of minutes, and make the sauce. This can take some time, depending on the amount of artistry that goes into it, but I think I shall approach it more as a whitewash job than an exercise in subtle brushwork.

I fling the chunks of lamb into the huge copper pan and watch them sizzle. Not too brown, too much colour but sufficiently long in the pan to be just cooked through to the middle: that is the secret. I prod them, as Roux taught me to, but I might as well have asked them how they felt for all that I gleaned from a push with a finger. Experienced chefs can tell the exact moment of cooking by squeezing a chunk of meat. All I do is burn my fingers.

Mark's first course has been whisked away on its silver tray, and superb it looked. Rich red lobster arranged between pink slices of salmon. He sliced a lump of one of the left-overs and shoved it in my mouth. Heaven.

The lamb is done. Chris says so. We're going to be spot on time. Blanc's team are way behind; they've still got their first course to fiddle with. The girl in the Sharrow Bay team has a panful of hot sugar and is creating with it. Nico's team are out of sight, but not out of our minds.

Roux suddenly haunts Chris and Mark. They fear disaster if I try to cook anything else, and so in the nicest possible way they give me a 'lift', a helping hand – more of a takeover really.

The white wine swills around the lamb pan. In goes the lamb stock, boiled till it thickens.

'Get me the muslin strainers,' cries Chris and in my dizzy state my hand goes automatically towards the rum bottle.

I arrange my chunks of meat in a pile in the centre of the silver dish. It looks for all the world like something from a dogfood commercial. The stuffed vegetables are scattered around it and Chris' perfect sauce is poured round that. We're only a minute late. Other teams haven't got their lamb out of the oven yet. There's time for a breather.

'The oven!' we all cry and throw the door open to find twenty of the saddest and crispest quenelles you have ever seen. It was just like Christmas dinner at home; something always gets forgotten in the oven. But it's too late now. The judges have the dish, and whatever the forcemeat might have added we shall never know.

I know it sounds immodest, but in the end we all thought it was a good dish. An artist is never the best critic of his own work, though; a dog's dinner to us might well be to the judge's perfect taste. All we could do was wait.

As it turned out, we didn't win. But we came close – we were runners-up. To this day I reckon the rissoles would have won it for us, but as far as I know they're still in the oven.

As for the other dishes, and especially Nico's winning dish of chopped lamb served as a large *vol-au-vent*, I have no idea what they tasted like. I never got the chance to see any of them again. Presumably they ended up in the swill bin.

I hear there's a pig going around somewhere with a huge smile on his face.

Horse
and
Courage

Horse and Courage

A grey May day on a flat Norfolk field. A Mercedes car parked on the edge gave its lone occupant a commanding view across the full width of the field. She was watching carefully from behind heavy black-rimmed spectacles, occasionally taking notes on a pad which rested on her tweedy lap. It was me she was watching, examining and dissecting, and it was very uncomfortable. I could feel her stare even from the other end of this ten-acre field.

And so could my horses: two Hungarian greys of enormous dignity, harnessed to a glossy black carriage with leather harness polished to a shine more dazzling than on the day it was made. A pair of thin leather reins, the width of dog-leads but six times as long, connected my hands to the horses' mouths, and that is how I controlled them. These leather ribbons are a tenuous connection, and could hardly be said to represent the enormous bond between me and these two animals – a mutual feeling that had grown in as short a time as three months. These two horses had become part of my life, a major part of it, since I had first been introduced to them and told that my task was to learn to drive them to competition standard and emulate the skills of the stage-coach drivers (or 'whips', as they were called) of Dickensian coaching days in a modern contest. And what's more, I was beginning to feel I could do it. My God, I was proud of myself and my horses as we manoeuvred round that flat Norfolk field, showing how we could turn and twist, stop and walk and trot at the lightest command – well, almost always.

The aged tweedy lady bundled herself out of the equally aged Mercedes with the help of a shooting stick, used more as a walking aid than a seat. White hair flowed as she walked, and the cigarette in its black holder was cast aside as she eventually arrived in the centre of the field where the two horses and I had come to a smart halt.

'Sloppy!' she declared. 'Sloppy!' she repeated, looking me square in the eye. 'Those horses have got all the go of two milk-float ponies and you're sitting there as if tomorrow will do, and tomorrow *won't* do.'

This was Cynthia Haydon on top crushing form. Mrs Haydon (as she is respectfully known to all competitors) breathes a fiery contempt for drivers who do not measure up to her exacting standards, and is quick to pour cold water on feeble efforts at horse-driving. But she is respected for it. A mean whip herself, with a team of four high-stepping, highly spirited Hackney horses, she had a reputation long before many of today's drivers knew their martingales from their breechings. She went on to criticise the way I changed the pace of the horses from trot to walk and back again. Even the way I sat wasn't good enough for her.

'You look like a sack of potatoes . . .' and the criticism flowed.

Why should it have worried me? Doesn't a series of endeavours such as these give the reporter a skin as thick as any horse hide? Isn't criticism all grist to the mill, to be taken up and learned from, and to give onlookers and readers an insight?

It was just that this time, everything was different. I fumed as I took my punishment. Not because she was wrong, or because I had an over-inflated notion of my developing skills, but because I was proud of those two horses, proud as any father might be of his children. If anyone was going to call them milk-float ponies it was going to be me, and not some tweedy dame chewing on a cigarette-holder. I cared.

Then there was John Parker to consider. John was my tutor, the man who had taken on his shoulders the Herculean task of converting me into a horseman. Me, a creature whose equestrian activity was confined to a seaside donkey-ride thirty years ago. John had worked on me, and with me, and I fumed for him too.

Under Mrs Haydon's withering scorn John was raging as well, for the horses and for me. Not that it's easy to tell when John Parker is rattled. His is an immobile face not really used to smiling and a perfect match for one of his favourite carriages – a horse-drawn hearse. If a Christmas-card artist had to draw a coachman, he would turn out like John Parker. Sharp features, eyes hooded, a timeless face; his nose and chin are Mr Punch reborn. He uses few words, but uses them to deadly effect. With an effort, in front of Mrs Haydon, he kept them to himself.

John cared as much as I did. In a matter of a few weeks, a solid triangular bond had been forged: John, myself and the horses.

On our first meeting, there was no reason to believe that any bond might form between us. On the contrary, there was much suspicion on all sides. John was naturally suspicious of anyone who sought to take up the sacred reins that only he liked to hold; and my reservations about 'horsey folk' were legion.

My first visit to Swingletree Stables was in early September. A few battered carriages littered the stable-yard, victims of a season's hard campaigning. John had a tired look too, but not from weariness; it is the way he always looks when there is doubt at the back of his mind. On this occasion, his doubts were about me.

'I'm like a horse,' John stated. 'I don't like pigs and I don't like wind and neither do my horses.'

Behind him, a dozen white horses' heads appeared over the half-doors of their stables, steamy breath just visible in the chilly air. They sensed their master's curiosity and were making their own minds up about me.

'Have you ever driven a horse?' John asked, and drew on his miniature cigar.

'No, never,' I replied.

'Have you ever ridden one?' he asked.

'No, never,' I replied again, lamely.

'That's no hardship, I suppose,' he said after some consideration, 'but you've got to get one thing in your head. These horses . . .' they were all looking my way now, obediently emphasising their master's point, '. . . have got brains. They think as well as you do and that's why you've got to work as a team with the horses.'

I glanced round in case they were nodding with approval.

'Do they know I'm a beginner?' I asked.

'They know exactly how much you know before you even touch the reins. You've got to gain their confidence in you. There's no point in thinking it's easy because it ain't. It's 'ard.' And he gave me a long, hard look from under the brim of his brown horseman's trilby.

The trouble is, it looks terribly easy to drive a horse (or in my case two since I had been set the task of driving a pair). It is as deceptively easy as say, getting notes out of a harp. But there is more to making music than plucking strings and there is more to driving horses than pulling on reins.

Introductions over, John took me for a drive. I sat on his left on what is known as the box seat, the raised platform on which the driver sits, and watched his hand carefully. No great tugging or pulling, no sudden jerks like the stage-coach drivers of Wells Fargo, no shouting of 'Yah' or cracking of whips; just a subtle twist of wrist and finger with an occasional tensing of the arm – like making music.

'It's more like fishing,' he said, 'you get a feeling. I know exactly when to pull. I can turn these horses by just twisting my hand.'

And he did. There and then. No fuss, no pulling. Just a flick of his wrist almost too subtle to see and they spun round and were heading the other way. Complete control.

We arrived at Wingfield village green and, in the shadow of the moated castle (it was the deep water rather than the castle that first caught my attention; there's nothing like driving a carriage to make you ditch-conscious), John handed me the reins and moved over to put me in the driving seat. One of the young girl grooms got down to hold the horses, which felt rather as if your driving instructor had put a wedge under the wheels while he nervously showed you the hill start. The reins travel all the way from your hand to the bit in the horse's mouth. That makes about twelve feet of leather down each side – no small weight. Halfway along, the rein splits into two and each goes to the left-hand side of each horse's mouth. The other rein also splits into two and each piece goes to the right-hand side of the mouth. That way, two reins can control two horses.

'Don't let go or you're in dead trouble,' John warned.

I tried. 'Gee-up' as a starting signal. I might as well have said please, for all the effect it had.

'You don't listen. We don't say "gee-up". We say "walk on".'

I tried it. It worked. It wasn't the most inspired or tidy departure that two horses had ever made but at least we were mobile.

'Keep talking to them . . . *keep talking*,' I could hear John saying.

What do you say to two horses whose names you don't even know? So I told them to walk on again. But they were walking already. I told them to wooah! but they just lumbered on. So I urged them to walk on again. But what was the point; they were doing exactly as they wished. I got annoyed. After all, I wasn't doing anything that John Parker hadn't done when he was driving – I was holding the reins in the same way. But they did what *he* told them and ignored *me*. I couldn't see why, and felt a fool.

We lumbered round in circles for a good fifteen minutes when we should really have been going in straight lines. John's grooms were never far away in case I dropped the reins in exasperation, or through fatigue, and the horses bolted for home. Then I caught sight of John, lighting up another cigar and grinning broadly.

'You were set up, boy!' he called and jumped back on to the box seat, taking the reins from me. 'I gave you the most difficult pair of horses I've got. You've got to be in this job for months before you can drive these two in a straight line.' He was enjoying his little joke mightily.

And, strangely, so was I, for there was a quality in John Parker's grin that told me we had crossed a watershed; never once had I blamed the horses. I had known that any deficiencies in their performance were due to my bungling. John likes people who respect his horses.

The first driving event I ever watched was at Windsor, on a manicured fifty-acre carpet of grass normally reserved for princes to play polo. On this occasion, however, it was the National Carriage Driving Championships.

'Where's the crowd?' I asked John.

'They're here!' he replied and I looked around. There were about six people on a stand looking at events in the ring and at least a dozen more, strolling around, working the creases out of their scarcely worn waxed jackets. Driving is no spectator sport. This was an event for competitors, and you could safely bet that anyone on the field that day was connected with an entry in some way.

There appeared to be two classes of competitor. One smartly dressed, polished and bedecked with leather finery; the other grubby, muddy and sweaty after a hard day's work. But, as John explained to me, they are really the same people. The competition is divided into three phases, each requiring a different get-up, and the smartest-looking ones were probably still in the first phase: presentation and dressage.

Presentation is really the battle of the Brasso bottles. Judges are looking for evidence of liberal application of spit and polish to horses, harness, and carriages. They'll lift cushions to check for dust, look for mud on the driver's shoes and examine the parts of buckles you can't normally see in the hope of catching sloppy competitors. But drivers are getting too good – they know all the judges' tricks and so the judges have to come up with new ones. They'll be asking drivers to open wide so they can check their fillings next.

Dressage is where the drivers start to show their skill. The rules state at which pace you should be going – walking, trotting, fast trot and so on – and during the test, which lasts for eight minutes, drivers have to show how well their horses will stand still, and even reverse in a straight line. Again, most of this is lost on the untrained eye. They're all pretty good and it seems to be only the slightest fault that separates those from the top from those lower down the score sheet. This is where that wretched Mercedes car is mostly likely to be seen; the one that is the mobile home of Mrs Haydon, the toughest of dressage judges.

'It's all to do with dignity,' said John. 'People have got to be able to go home saying, "That looked nice." That's why you've got to do your own cleaning . . .' and he tailed off as his eye was taken by a group of keen-eyed spectators who had gathered in a clump of trees on the rougher ground that surrounded the show ring.

I could hear the thunder of hooves heading our way. We had moved into the second phase of the competition: the marathon. This is an endurance test of man and horses: twenty miles of rough cross-country driving through fields and forest, across rivers and through deliberately placed hazards. These might be a slalom of immovable oil drums to be negotiated, or a series of gate posts and fences that have to be treated like a maze, but whatever the hazard might be, you can be certain that it will be tight, with very little room for error. Speed counts too. The fastest drivers through the hazards tend to be the eventual winners.

The hazard we were going to see today was the sandpit. A sort of bomb crater with steep banks of sandy earth and a few small trees bravely sprouting in it.

'This will give you something to think about,' warned John.

A series of barrels had been placed in the bottom of the pit, and it required a series of S-shaped movements to get the horses through. No room for error and, with the steep sides and tight turns, much scope for disaster.

'They build these courses hard,' said John, remembering the last time he had seen this, from the box seat and not from the ringside. 'You've got to drive through with no assistance, you can't get off the carriage and neither can your grooms.'

Four powerful brown horses appeared between the trees and with hardly a falter they trotted down the crumbling sides of the sandpit. Obedience was essential. If they didn't stop at the bottom they would crash into the barrel stop too soon and would not be able to make the tight turn that would get them through quickly and on to the rest of the course. There was no shouting or screaming, just an orderly placing of those horses by the driver in exactly the position he wanted them. A tug on a rein and the ones in front would start to turn, another tug and the ones behind would follow. Reins pulled back could reverse all four horses and effectively execute a three-point turn. Masterful. The crowd roared. John smiled. My mouth dropped open.

This sport is full of contrasts. Wealthy owners with coach-built horseboxes will park alongside less well-heeled competitors whose horses have travelled in a converted double-decker bus. Grooms may spend nights under canvas, owners in the luxury of American motor-homes. All harness will be spotlessly clean, but some will have richly carved brasswork for decoration and some will be plain and simple. One driver might have a fine team of horses, imported from Spain or even Hungary, while his neighbour might be justly proud of a pair of black hairy ponies just down from a winter on a Cumbrian hillside. But the common enemies unite them: the marathon course and the beady eye of the judge. Champions will dispense advice to newcomers, and the less well equipped will find it no trouble to borrow from those who have more than two of everything.

These driving events have a family feeling, so it was less of a surprise to find the Duke of Edinburgh, normally remote and aloof, down in the midst of it. No visible security, no press spokesman on hand; just the Duke, wandering, greeting, grumbling about the dressage judge, cautioning about a hazard, dispensing wisdom freely. And no bowing and scraping in return, either. All men are equal when set behind horses with a competition to drive.

However, I had not been long enough in this game to be entirely without inhibition when I was invited by John to join him and the Duke by the dressage ring. What should

I do with my hat? I'd taken to wearing a flat cap, but do you take it off, do you raise it briefly? I took it off and then held it so long in my hand that it would have been rude to replace it. So I carried it for the next hour like a man at a lengthy funeral.

There is no limit to the Duke's enthusiasm for other people's errors. He will point out every deviation from an otherwise perfect performance. If two or three hours watching the dressage is not enough, he will turn on his portable video camera and record a few competitors to while away the hours back at the Palace. He will tut-tut and draw in his breath when some error has been made, usually one totally undetectable to an other than experienced eye. Quite frankly I hadn't a clue what he meant most of the time.

'I think the dressage is the most difficult bit of the whole contest,' he told me, talking through his teeth in the manner of his popular image. 'Every time you do it, you try to do it with precision and something goes wrong. There's a lot of luck in it.'

I glanced down at the programme, which gave details of the movements required for the dressage test, and counted at least twenty which all had to be done in the right order and with no outside prompting. I asked him if he ever got confused? How could you possibly practise it at home?

'Get a carpet [this was clearly an order], preferably a prayer mat,' and he jumped to his feet to demonstrate, 'and you run up and down the carpet saying to yourself "I'm walking" or "I'm trotting" or "I'm extending" . . .'

He paused to bark at a handful of photographers whose collective clicking of cameras sounded like the hammering of woodpeckers.

'Are you all mad?' he barked at them.

'Concentrate all the time,' he spun round to look me in the eye. 'You've got an animal in front of you and it's got its own point of view and you've got to figure out how it's going to react at any given time. It's no good thinking he's all right because you're just trotting down the road. That's when he'll spot a dog, or something else, and he'll be away and you'll end up in the ditch.' He spun round.

'Look at what that fool's doing. Look. *Look!*' he nearly screamed. I looked. Seemed perfect to me. That's the problem with dressage.

There is a process of parcelling a horse in leather; it's called harnessing-up. This was to be my first and most important lesson. It was John's intention that I should be a complete whip, a total horseman; not simply a grand-prix driver with no knowledge of how to change a wheel, or whatever the equestrian equivalent might be. At this point, Susan Townsend appeared on the scene. To be accurate, not much of her appeared until she dropped a huge pile of black leather harness that she had lugged a hundred yards from house to stables. It would have been a burden for most men, but no problem for this slight blonde who is John's partner at Swingletree Stables. Susan is most often to be found in the middle of a pile of harness, for she is the harness-maker. Her slender fingers drive massive needles through leather and cut thick pieces of hide without faltering: she is tough as nails, devoted to horses, and a first-class driver herself.

She began parcelling the horses up.

'Collar on first. It's an old coaching tradition. If anything goes on before the collar, it's bad luck,' said Susan.

Collars are the heavy bit. Oval in shape, they rest on the horse's shoulders and, as it is from the collar that the horse pulls, it's got to fit.

'Put it on upside down, or you'll never get it over her head.'

I was forcing it now, trying to squeeze the narrow top of the collar over the bulging but patient eyes of the poor animal.

'Turn it upside down,' said Susan more emphatically. 'Drop it back down the neck and twist it so that it's the right way up.'

I corkscrewed the thing round and it came to rest on the horse's shoulders. So far so good.

The old grey mare (who wasn't what she used to be, after my clumsy harnessing attempt) looked on contemptuously.

'Don't let her stand on the harness, she'll break it!' warned Susan.

'Next the pad and crupper! Lift her tail and stuff it through. Tighten the girth, not too tight. Now the belly band . . . pick up your traces . . . make sure they're the right way up.'

And it gets ever more complicated. Harness is designed to be quickly removable in the event of accidents, so all buckles are accessible from the outside of the horse. That means the near side and off-side horses wear different harness. You learn to spot which is which after a couple of hundred times of getting it wrong.

'You've forgotten the martingale . . .' cried Susan, pointing to a loop hanging down between the mare's front legs.

'When you throw a rein over a horse, you shout "rein coming over" to tell grooms on the other side to stand clear,' added Susan.

I picked up the leather strap, coiled it in my hand and, with the force of a weather forecaster predicting a deluge, I cried, '*Rein* coming over!'

'Sssssh!' urged Susan, and the old grey mare shifted uneasily on her four big feet.

The shows were fun, but the days at Swingletree Stables were the best. They rapidly became less of a labour and more of a pleasure, and indeed became the most vivid part of my life. I would stroll around my home in London and come across my driving gloves or old duffle coat and smell the sweat of a working horse or the freshness of a bale of hay. Or I might open my wallet in Shepherd's Bush and draw out a few pieces of straw; the odour that filled the air was of the muck I'd been shovelling off the stable floor and it reminded me that 'out with the horses' was where I wanted to be.

My visits to Norfolk would start and end with cups of good strong tea. There were a good few in-between too, for my visits were on shortening autumn days and we would sit in John's kitchen waiting for the fog to lift or the sun to melt the thin but dangerous glaze of frost on the roads. John would tell me the rights and wrongs of the driving world, and it would be Susan who would put down her tea first and galvanise us into action by lugging harness across to the stable yard.

I remember the smells best of all. The tack room, with at least fifty sets of top quality harness to fit everything from Shetland ponies to John's prize Spanish stallion, had a scent all its own: rich and dark to match the deep black and brown of the leather, but with a sharp cutting edge to it which I always associated with the gleaming brasswork. Then there were the stables, where I learnt that there is nothing offensive about horse manure. To go into a stable on a chilly morning is to enter a warm and comforting world. Those who can't stand the smell are missing a treat; for me it ranks alongside the Havana cigar or the applewood fire as one of the great smells of all time.

Some mornings, I would chat to the horses before the serious tea-drinking began. Early morning in a large stable is a peaceful time, with the sound of gentle munching and the rustle of birds flying in and out to find seeds fallen from the hay. A robin might perch on a stable door, keeping an eye on affairs, and the horses would eye him back.

I remember poor old Rubillio – one-eyed, head always on one side in search of a pat, a tickle or best of all a mint. He was described to me as 'bad on his feet'. Then there was Gyorgy – a big girl, big in the head anyway, but with a little less brainpower than some of the others, John would say. 'She's not quite certain which foot to put down in which order. Legs all over the place, that's Gyorgy!'

Then there were the clever ones, Pandur and Level – the ones who recognised beginners when they saw them and took advantage. Like a row of Chinamen, John's horses all looked the same at first, and it was quite a few months before I could instantly tell one from the other. Being Hungarian horses, they all had unusual names. There was Bojtar, which means 'little prince'; Rubillio, which means 'policeman'; and there was one called Henry, whatever Henry might be Hungarian for.

But two of them were becoming special friends: Agy and Bollio. These were the two that John thought best suited to me and they would be the pair that I would eventually drive in the competition.

Even his greatest fans would tell you that Bollio was not the most delicate of animals. He was one of the few you could spot a mile off due to the exceptional broadness of his head, and his eyes were in a permanent state of half-closure, as if he was in need of a good night's sleep. He was a miserable sod, too. You only had to come near him with the harness for him to chew at his stable door in protest and generally let it be known that life was too much of an effort for him. But once in harness, there was no stronger or more willing horse. Brave too; he proved it over and over again in competition. So conscientious was he that any scolding aimed at other horses would always fall upon his ears and he would double his efforts to try and make amends. After a couple of months I recognised him for a great horse.

Agy, the old grey mare, was a great horse too but less giving than Bollio. She always showed great indifference to the harness and would delay any attempt you might make to coax her into a bridle. John taught me a way of doing it which involved inserting a thumb in the horse's mouth to force it open, but even then, Agy only opened her teeth just far enough to allow the cold steel bit to slip between. But she went well for me, and if she flagged a little there was always Bollio to take up the challenge.

When you are driving your horses they seem a long way away: they are on the ends of two strings, and that is all the control you have except for the whip, a rather crude accelerator which you hold in your right hand. You also have your voice, which has more influence than you might believe, but still there are times when you feel no more in control than a puppeteer directing his marionettes through lengths of twine. But horses have brains, and even as they amble along they are thinking, probably faster than you are. It is rare for the same thought to cross your mind as crosses theirs, and so any temptation to enjoy the passing scenery is to be avoided. This was John's recurrent theme: concentration. My brain would ache after only a couple of hours' driving.

The first thing a driver has to do before setting off is to check the harness, especially if he has done it himself. He then takes the reins in his left hand and mounts the carriage. After this I would sit, ostensibly carrying out more checks, but in reality just putting off the moment of shouting 'Walk on!'

I could never guess what would happen when the horses took their first pace forward. Sometimes one horse might set off slightly before the other and the carriage would slew round, rather as if the left-hand side of a car had set off before the right. Then there would be days when the horses didn't want to move at all – dozy days when munching hay seemed far more attractive than plodding a regular five-mile circuit. What was I to do then?

'Give 'em a tap up the bum with the whip . . .' John would urge.

But how much of a tap? Too hard and they're away like frightened racehorses, too gentle and you're wasting your time.

It's surprisingly easy to confuse a horse, as I quickly discovered. In his mutterings under his breath, John, when he was driving, would be preparing his horses for what he was about to ask of them. He might mumble 'come by' or 'come over', and they knew then that they were about to make a turn, but a sudden jab in the mouth with the bit, as administered by me in my early days, was as much use as trying to teach a child to cross a road by pulling its arm. I would end up with the horses looking this way and that and wondering where they might be going next. Poor old Agy and Bollio.

I learnt to watch their ears carefully, and I was always well rewarded. You can tell a happy child from the look on its face, and a driver can tell a happy horse from the position of his ears. They flick, sometimes in rhythm with your voice. A distant sound, maybe a bird or an unexpected crunch from under a carriage wheel, would have them flicking backwards and forwards like radar scanners. But generally speaking, ears forward is good news and ears permanently back is not.

'Not bad, not bad,' offered John after our first lesson. 'I usually have to take the reins at some stage during the first lesson, but you did all right, boy!'

And I did even better – John said so over and over again. I was entranced with enjoyment and appreciation; I was loving it.

Most of it anyway – dressage wore a bit thin on occasions, perhaps because it is the most exacting test of driving skill. The cross-country part of the competition tests your nerve and stamina, but dressage feels more like a driving test. You are asked to perform, with the utmost precision, movements that you know you might never have to do again. The judge has to be satisfied and the dressage judge, you remember, is Mrs Haydon. Horses get bored with dressage too. After a couple of runs at the eight-minute test, they begin to pre-empt every move and you will find that the wide, sweeping curves you had intended have suddenly had the corner cut off them. Ears might be back too, out of frustration at having constantly to perform within the confines of an arena; drivers' tempers shorten too.

It was being able to have only an occasional practice which was the greatest frustration. At least with a car, if you don't get the three-point turn right you can have another go, but if you try to drive horses in circles more than a couple of times tempers shorten: mine, John's as well, but principally Agy and Bollio's.

Still, things improved. Was it my imagination, or were those two grand horses beginning to work for me instead of just with me? Were we developing that all-important bond of which John had talked so much, the link between driver and horse that is more essential than the reins themselves? I think we were. Initially, it was a sentimental attraction. I looked forward to seeing their faces peering over the stable door, and even if Bollio was showing his lack of enthusiasm by grinding his teeth on the wooden door-jamb, at least I knew it was 'just his way'. In other words, I knew those two horses and fondly began to imagine that they were beginning to know me too.

I was also learning to divide my concentration, for although I still had to consider carefully any movement of hand or wrist, part of my mind was also able to dwell on Agy and Bollio and know the mood they were in. Had Bollio cheered up now that he had the cow-parsley to sniff as he trotted between the hedgerows? Was Agy in one of her lazy moods and holding back a little to allow all the work to fall on her partner? That was a favourite trick of hers, and I was getting to know them all by now. We were forming a great team, a team of which John was beginning to be proud. He had not only schooled the horses, he'd schooled their driver too.

Then Agy nearly died. No one who saw the accident could fail to be moved by the look on her face as she lay, half submerged in water, pinned to the river bed by a horse on top of her and the full weight of the carriage. No one who saw the bravery of the other horses would forget the valiant way they stood their ground with no hint of panic; knowing that one of their friends was in trouble. John was the driver. I was standing on the rear of the carriage, as groom. John's partner Susan was with us too and so was Roger, John's navigator round the tough cross-country course at the Royal Windsor Horse Show. John was driving his team of four horses in competition, and the team was going well. My friends Agy and Bollio were the pair nearest to the carriage and the two in front were another pair I had driven on occasion, Pandur and Level.

We had successfully negotiated five of the eight hazards with great aplomb. Roger was an airline pilot by profession and was using fast mental stopwatch calculations to ensure that we were at the right point on the course at the right time. We trotted smartly over the top of a small hill, John's four perfectly groomed white horses cascading down the slope like a waterfall. Then came the water hazard. Nothing very difficult about it – just a trot through the three-foot-deep water and a slight bend before climbing out the other side. John collected his horses and brought them back to a slower trot.

'Go on . . . go on . . .' he urged, knowing he had their trust and that if he told them he thought it was safe to go on, they would do so. The two horses in the lead cast the water aside with their feet and bravely went on. Agy and Bollio followed behind. Halfway through, we were going well and our minds turned from concern over the water to worrying about which way we were to go after that. Then I felt a lurch as the carriage came to a sudden halt. There was a gasp from the crowd and I saw people running towards us. I froze. I couldn't see what had happened but my trust in John told me that there was no problem he could not sort out, so I stood there.

Then Susan screamed. She had jumped down and found the water deeper than the three feet we had been led to believe. I jumped down too and saw the full scale of the disaster. Agy was down in the water, her head hardly above the surface and not able to take a breath without taking in water as well. In falling, she had brought Bollio on top of her, and he was now kicking in fright. The two lead horses, Pandur and Level, were frozen as if standing to attention. Susan was wading through the water as best she could. She was vital, since her intricate knowledge of the now-tangled harness was the only thing that was going to sort out this mess. Roger had the courage and wit to hold Agy's head above water so she could breathe. The crowd were screaming now and helpers were wading into the water, some offering expert advice and others, who should have known better, only adding to the tangle.

'Get their heads . . . get their heads . . .' John shouted again and again. I could have cried from the frustration of not knowing what to do next. I helped Susan drag out the pole which was lying across Bollio's poor back and which had been taking the full weight of the carriage. This team, this finely tuned collection of horses was a wreck. It had ticked as perfectly as a clock and now lay like a pile of broken springs. I could not bear to see my old friends, sodden and miserable but bravely standing their ground.

I could not see how Agy would survive. Bollio started to take fright and was kicking out. Susan was first to unharness the leaders and lead them to the water's edge. Then, slowly and surely, Agy and Bollio emerged muddy and bleeding from the water. We do not know how or why it happened. Did Agy suddenly take fright and leap into the air and tangle herself in the harness on landing? Perhaps.

We led them back to the horsebox, Susan in tears, John solemn.

'It's not fair,' said John with look of a man who had come close to seeing his family wiped out, 'it's not fair on the horses. Remember, Paul, the horses didn't ask to come here.'

I had spent six months getting to know those two horses, Agy and Bollio, and all that work had now vanished into the mud at the bottom of the lake at Windsor. There seemed little chance that they would be fit enough for my competition, which was only a month away. I could always drive another pair of John's horses, but with none of the style and confidence with which I handled these two.

Back home, it became clear that although Agy had appeared to take the worst of it and was gratefully accepting all the sympathy, it was Bollio who had silently and courageously taken most of the strain. It was painful to watch them try to flex their torn and bruised muscles as they took gentle exercise in John's indoor arena.

My mind now split: only half looking backwards to that dreadful accident, the other looking forwards to the driving event at which I was to compete – the Norwich Union Horse Driving Trials at Wramplingham in Norfolk. John's admonition that 'the horses didn't ask to come' reminded me constantly of the driver's responsibility to his animals as well as to himself and passengers. When I discussed this with John, he would flatter me by telling me, 'you're becoming a real horseman'. Whatever, I decided that winning was not of importance; driving Agy and Bollio safely round the course was my main objective, if Agy would willingly go round another marathon course with the accident still fresh in her mind. If she wasn't willing, neither John nor I was going to push her.

With the two horses only doing gentle exercise to rebuild their strength, the long hours round the Brasso tin began. Long for me and even longer for John's grooms, led by Carol and Isobel, who had a way with boot polish and Brasso that made the Army look like beginners.

It was over the harness-cleaning sessions that I would hear other tales of doom and disaster: drivers being knocked out as their carriages overturned and driving on as soon as their sight lost its blurriness . . . the time when the reins broke . . . when a wheel came off . . . when a pair of horses met a swarm of bees . . . and so on. 'The horses didn't ask to come . . .' echoed around my head.

Competitors are allowed to walk or take cars round the cross-country course the day before the event; they can make a plan of attack that way. There was little driving round my course except by Land Rover – it had become a mud-bath. Weeks of constant rain, followed by a cloud-burst the night before, had swollen rivers and ditches, which had overflowed to, if not submerge some of the obstacles, ensure at least that the first horses through them would churn them into a sea of mud.

John was very quiet, and the more he saw the quieter he became. The first fifteen miles were going to be very difficult, if not impossible, through the sludge. His heart clearly sank when he saw the man-made obstacles at the end of the course: tight, intricate mazes of logs, poles and up-ended sewer pipes. Flags and hedges had been placed with all the cunning that the course-builders could muster.

Then came the water hazard. After Windsor, water was very much on our minds, and John and I stood on the bank looking at the torrent which was usually a stream. 'This is more difficult than the World Championships . . .' John said, staring in disbelief at the water obstacle. Other top team-drivers were shaking their heads, too.

Presentation is the first part of the contest; it is a game between grooms and judges while drivers just sit and are examined like so much window-dressing. Good grooms know all the judge's tricks and, thanks to John, I had superb grooms; brass and leather had never sparkled so brightly, horses never looked whiter. Drivers have to look smart too. Mud on the boots will be marked down and suitable dress is considered to be a suit and grey top hat. Judges have marked competitors down whose grooms have sewn a tail-coat button off-centre, and they'll even drop you marks if the flower in your buttonhole is wilting. Pity the poor drivers whose carriage-lamp candles are brand new – new candles are more difficult to light than ones that have been lit before, so new candles are considered by judges to be unroadworthy.

'Thank you,' came a call from beneath a distant bowler hat (all male judges wear bowlers) and that signified that the presentation was over. I jogged the horses round in circles to try and keep them warm: it was the dressage contest in fifteen minutes. Susan was to be my groom, and in her smartest livery of black coat, top hat, white breeches and polished boots, she sat in the back of the carriage too nervous to say a word.

The hooter sounded: our signal to enter the arena. At that moment, I spotted the dreaded Mercedes – the one that had shadowed, vulture-like, my early attempts at dressage. It was Mrs Haydon's car and she was the judge today.

I trotted up to the centre mark in the arena, called to the horses to stop, and put my foot firmly on the brake; we slithered to a standstill. I swapped the whip from right to left hand, still holding the reins, and removed my top hat in salute. The Mercedes did not reply. I caught sight of John standing by the side of the ring; he looked in a dreadful state, like a man watching his own funeral.

We started to do the turns and bends. I could see John, concentrating as hard as if he were driving. The one-handed circle worked, much to my amazement. Then round the other way, and that worked too! We were back

on the centre mark now and came to a halt in preparation
for the reverse, the stage in the test where a driver must
show his skill in moving carriage and horses backwards in
a straight line. It is far more difficult than it looks.

'Right . . . Agy and Bollio . . .' I whispered to them,
and with not only their total attention but mine as well, I
slowly pulled my handful of rein towards me.

'Come back . . . come back . . .' I urged them with
every step. They were going straight. I urged them some
more and back they came in a faultless line.

We all sighed, and went forward again to finish the rest
of the test.

The score sheet made grim reading: halt crooked . . .
lost impulsion . . . half circle too big . . . circles irregular
. . . hands not held high enough. It read like a commentary
on a bad accident. But the score was hardly believable. It
put me into second place. Me! My first event and I'm up
there with the drivers who have been playing this game for
years. God bless the lady in the Mercedes.

John took me to one side, 'We've proved you can drive,'
he told me, looking at ease for the first time for many
days. 'The dressage is the real test of driving ability.
Whatever happens in the marathon, you've proved you
can do it.' And he gave me a good slap on the back.

It poured with rain overnight. The water hazard, the
one that worried us all, was deeper than ever. Would it be
too deep for Agy; and what if she took fright, as she had at
Windsor, but with me holding the reins this time?

We collected our referee, who sits beside the driver and
checks that the correct course has been taken with no
short cuts. They also watch for breaks of pace; it will cost
you marks if you're trotting when you should be walking,
cantering when you should be trotting.

The starter counted us down. I called 'Walk on' to Agy
and Bollio and away we went.

'Just imagine you're driving at home,' urged John who
was standing behind me and was to be my navigator.

We settled into a gentle trot, both horses going well and
their driver feeling on good form. We were well on time for

the second section of the course, John checking us against his stopwatch all the way. The groom can give you directions, shout, scream, do what he likes as long as he doesn't touch the whip, the reins or the handbrake. John, behind me, was itching to do all those things.

Section A completed with no penalties and no breaks of pace. Next: the two-mile walk. It is like swimming against a tide or walking backwards up an escalator. You urge the horses to walk out without breaking into a trot and costing you points. You can see the finishing line ahead, and they can see it too so you hold them back; and then you get behind time so you urge them on some more. They break pace, another mark lost.

'Keep talking to them,' John reminded me.

'Walk on Agy . . . walk on . . .'

We were late. Marks lost on that section.

Then the fast trot, about five miles. The horses went as fast as they could, pulling as hard as could be asked of them as the ground slithered under each footfall. Agy broke into the occasional canter and I cursed her. Bollio pulled and pulled like no horse ever had before; he pressed forward, dragging the load that Agy occasionally avoided. We slithered on and off the tracks, too close to the ditches for any comfort.

'Concentrate . . . right rein . . . *left* rein,' boomed John from behind me.

My reactions were slowing, the horses tiring; we were not halfway round yet. The referee clocked up some more penalties. I sweated some more.

Then another cursed walk section. We were all tired by now. I had less will to urge the horses on, and the horses were weary too – none of us had much physical and mental reserves to call upon. My left arm ached from the constant pull of this pair of horses, and my reactions had slowed. But the most gruelling part of the course was yet to come.

The hazards are a perverse combination of posts and ditches, trees and barrels, all placed by the course-builder to test a driver's control and a horse's courage. They are like a maze, but with optional routes through them. There's a safer, but longer, way through, which might be easier for the driver but take him longer and cost him points. There's also a quick and sneaky way through, but it calls for more driving skill because if you discover halfway through the hazard that you've bitten off more than you can chew you're stuck, and that will cost you more points than if you'd made a more stately progress through the infernal thing.

We approached the first. No problems between the first pair of poles, or even the second. I pulled on the left rein, urged them between another pair of posts and we were through. Through? Surely this was too easy. John slapped me on the back again, Agy and Bollio were told they were the finest horses ever to have walked the earth and with great confidence we set off for the next hazard.

The second was more difficult – built like a corridor with a kink in it and the whole thing little wider than the carriage. We got firmly stuck. This was one of those hazards where you had to be perfectly placed or you would not get through, and the mud ensured that wherever I placed the carriage it slithered into an impossible position of its own accord. John started to bellow at the horses, 'Get on . . . Get on . . .' Brute force was going to get us through this hazard. It did. Hazard three was a simple bridge and presented no problems except to provide us with an ominous glimpse of the river which was to form our next hazard: the water crossing. Throughout the day, drivers had been getting into trouble in the water hazard. Top drivers too, with years of experience behind them, not beginners with aching arms, flagging concentration and weary horses.

Agy was the one I had to concentrate on. 'Good girl . . . go on . . . go on . . .' I urged her every step of the way, down the slippery river bank and into the fast-running water that came halfway up her legs. Bollio did not flinch. 'Right rein, now your left . . .' shouted John from behind, my hands now beginning to move like a punch-drunk boxer. Each of John's orders was backed up by a thump to the appropriate shoulder. The horses came round the tight turns but not as quickly or as soon as they might have done if I had been a bit fresher in my mind. The crowd were silent.

We made the first turn round the up-ended drainage pipes, then the second. Only one more to go and the lousy water hazard would be over.

'Go on Agy . . . good girl Agy . . . *good girl* . . .' we were through.

'We've made it . . .' I nearly screamed and the horses, sensing the relief, broke into a spirited canter up the river bank and out of the hazard. The crowd roared too.

We were back in the race. We drove like hell through the rest of the hazards, scraping a few on the way through. Only one to go, now.

Another bowler-hatted figure came running towards us, shouting for us to stop. An earlier competitor was stuck in the last hazard and had to be helped out before we could attempt it. It was like running half-way round a marathon course and then being told to jog on the spot a few yards from the finish. John sharply turned everybody away who tried to come and keep us company. We had a momentum now and it was in danger of evaporating during this tedious wait; to lose it now would have cost us any chance of completing the course.

Into the last hazard: horses sensing that it was nearly over. Agy cheekily looked both ways as we trotted in, as if asking which way to go. The break had given me time to think: what a team we had become, me and the two horses and John. Only four months ago, none of us had met and here we were, charging across fields and tracks as one. We glided between the first pair of flags, then the second, and out. We had finished all the hazards and all that stood between us and the finish was a mile of routine cross-country driving.

'You're eliminated!' shouted a judge as we left the final hazard. We let it sink in and didn't say a word, John trying to remember in his muddled mind where we might have gone wrong. If the judge was right, it would mean we were out of the contest. I could only drive home now, like a robot. 'Good boys . . . good boys . . .' I would mutter over and over again, but not loud enough for the poor horses to hear; I was too tired to shout any more.

John was desolate when he remembered that final gate in the last hazard that we thought we had been through, but in fact had missed. John thought he had cost me the competition. But it didn't matter in the slightest. I had brought horses and carriage home in one piece. What did a competition matter now? I jumped down soon after crossing the finishing line and cried from relief and pride in the two horses, Agy and Bollio.

I rested my head on Bollio's broad nose, inhaling the sweaty smell of him that I had come to know so well over the months.

'You went in there like a soldier, a good old soldier . . .' I whispered to him, and fought back the tears of joy and relief.

They were also tears of sadness. Four of the happiest months of my life were almost at their end. I had discovered new loves, new friends, where I least expected to find them. I had opened a door into a whole new world, all through meeting John Parker and his horses. And now I had to close it again.

I watched Agy and Bollio walk up the ramp into the horsebox, only hay and water on their minds now. I was left with a silly collection of relics: a top hat, a pair of leather gloves and a pile of smelly old jackets and trousers. Never with a more heavy heart did I stuff it all into the back of the car, the aromatic scent of the horses surrounding me as I did so. I heard the engine of the horsebox start; I could not turn to watch it drive away.

John came up to me.

'If you want to drive again, boy, just you ring . . .' and he shook me by the hand.

I rang. And drove. And have done countless times ever since.

Hearts
and
Flaws

Hearts and Flaws

Like the apocryphal monkey, if I sit here long enough, hitting these typewriter keys, I shall churn out the works of Shakespeare. But what would be the point in that? Impressive perhaps, but hardly as lucrative as a thriller, or a ten-generation saga, or a romance. Shakespeare may have his literary plus-points, but he's got a long way to go before his sales figures match those of less worthy writers. And that's the sort of writing I'm interested in. I want to write a book that gets the 'hype', the sell that can persuade millions to buy it (if they read it, so much the better, but buying is sufficient). I once met a scholarly man who was writing a book. It was about the use of the subjunctive clause in *Hamlet*. Best of luck, mate. It was hardly going to propel him into the best-seller lists or on to the all-important chat shows. That's what I want – the big promotional tours. Not just Wogan and a bit of Radio 4, but Johnny Carson coast-to-coast, a whistle-stop tour of the Commonwealth and translation into ninety-seven languages; all of this culminating in a tearful farewell to England as I fly into enforced tax exile, or perhaps a senior position in a political party?

It's not an unusual fantasy for people in my job. If it weren't for the immediate task of reporting the latest meeting of the County Council or committing to print the first reactions of the Spot-the-Ball winner, many journalists, not unlike monkeys, believe that if they just sit down for long enough they too will become Freddie Forsyth, Dick Francis, or Barbara Cartland. I have chosen what I take to be the easiest option: I intend to write a romance.

I find it difficult to believe that the writing of romantic fiction is a gift given only to a few. Take this for example:

She sat up straight, but Jim's strong arms pulled her back against him. When his eyes came back to hers, there was warmth in them. His mouth curled wide and he began to laugh. Janice felt the red of pure happiness filling her face. The ache within her was beyond tears now.

I am sure I could do that. But where do I start? Certainly not by setting out on a 500-page novel. I have the sense to try the nursery slopes first, and so turn to the natural home of the romantic writer – a weekly magazine which claims to be 'famed for its fiction'. Famous for its slop, more like. Not that it's sloppily written or presented, far from it, but listen to this:

And then he looked beyond Becky and their eyes met. Locked in that brief breathless instant she knew it was going to be all right; knew that this time it had to be, knew they were meant for each other, knew that whatever their tempestuous relationship held in store, they would come together again, always, no matter how long it took.

You can call it what you like, but I call it slop. But a million people a week will coo and weep over it, and that's what counts when it's the million-dollar dream that is driving you on. If I can get a story in this magazine I shall be on the way to my goal. The magazine is called *Woman's Weekly*.

But first I needed an agent. Agents dirty their hands with money, leaving writers merely to soil their fingertips on the typewriter ribbons. Agents project themselves as the humble middlemen, although it is more usual for agents to visit their authors in Bentleys than the other way round. Agents sit on a fence that divides two rival factions; on the one hand is the writer – creative and unfettered by worldly considerations such as East Asian paperback royalties – and on the other are the romantic publishers, who are not benevolent institutions. They are into marketing, and some will meddle with the writer's sacrosanct words, invent whole chapters and story-lines, and only occasionally tell the writer they've done it.

And how does the agent behave? He milks both cows. He'll cream off the writer's talent and feed it, at a price, to the publisher. In return, he'll extract as much sustenance as he can from the publisher's purse to feed back to his poor writer, with a little nibble for himself on the way.

Herself, in my case: Carol Smith. Her friends call her 'pushy and beaky'. She is an ambitious, slightly built, fast-talking blonde with a declared confidence in the short story and in the potential of young, untried writers. She decided, early on in her career, that she would have a diamond ring for every manuscript she sold for a million dollars. After a couple of highly successful years, shortage of fingers forced her to stop. If that was what they meant by 'pushy', that was OK by me; who wants an agent who rushes home to his teddy bear when a publisher speaks to him sternly? As for 'beaky', as long as she was prepared to stick her nose into my manuscripts, I didn't give a damn what shape it might be.

Her office is also her home. A block of flats off Kensington High Street each with two doorbells: one for visitors, the other for servants. There were letters on her desk with House of Commons headings (who I wondered, was moonlighting?). In conversation, the words 'a million dollars' cropped up as often as you or I might say 'umm'.

Like a pupil asking teacher for the exam answers, I asked Carol for the formula.

'No,' she replied quickly and forcefully, 'there *isn't* a formula. If there were, you would just be sending the whole thing up. There are some subjects you should avoid of course – there's a formula in that sense.'

I listened very carefully and took good note.

'I think we've had too many stories with terminal illness. We've also had a lot of books about the world wars. Don't write about the *Titanic*, we've had enough of that. And don't write about the Jews, they're out of fashion at the moment.'

'What about heroes and heroines,' I asked softly, my eyes searching hers.

'No sex,' insisted Carol, severely. 'No sex whatsoever. If it's *Woman's Weekly* you'll get away with a kiss. The heroine has to be decent and straight and the hero has to be heroic in some way, although he can still be the boy next door.'

She carries a look that says, 'This is not going to be as easy as you thought, young man.'

'If you can dazzle yourself, it will work. It has to be a sort of gut thing. At the end of the day, when you've written it, a tear should come to your eye.'

And on that moving note I left. Wiser and worried, but with an agreement that she would look at my first efforts and advise.

You would expect *Woman's Weekly* to operate from a cosy little cottage: home-made jam bubbling away on the stove, cuddly toys being stuffed, and conversation just audible over the clack of knitting needles. In fact, the best-selling weekly magazine in the world is housed in a concrete wilderness on the south bank of the Thames halfway between the National Theatre and the Oxo Tower. Still, symbolically it is a perfect spot – a hint of literature and a dash of home cooking.

The two women I was to meet were in a bit of a flap. A grey-fringed, matronly lady was tutt-tutting over an article in the *Guardian* which had described her as grey-fringed and matronly. This turned out to be the editor, Brenda. Meanwhile, the other lady, Linda, seemed to be discreetly enjoying the joke. Linda is the fiction editor.

There is much insistence inside the business that there is no formula, no set line along which these stories must run. Carol Smith denied the existence of rules, and so did Linda and Brenda. And then, like Carol, they started to lay them down.

'Your story must have a happy ending, or at least the possibility of a happy ending. I'd have to say no to a story that didn't end happily,' said Brenda. 'Nobody's going to want to read 4,000 words, get involved with the characters and then some terrible holocaust happens and it all ends up in death and destruction.'

I took note of the compulsory happy ending. Having established that, I asked if crime or violence might come into the story, providing it all ended happily? Mugger and victim fall in love, that sort of thing.

'That is not the real world,' and Brenda leaned across her desk, put her head slightly to one side and raised her voice just a little to make her point. 'To the majority of people that isn't real at all. The real world is their family world and the family traditions that they still live by, and that's our readership. If you want to write for *Woman's Weekly*, that's what you've got to do.'

The bedroom is real, even to the readers of *Woman's Weekly*, one assumes. So, pushing my luck a bit, I suggested that bedroom scenes would be fine, as long as it all ended happily and was within the family?

No such luck. Linda joined in: 'We are exploring that period of time when two people meet and decide whether they're attracted to each other. What happens after the story is up to them . . . so lurid bedroom scenes will *not* figure in your story.'

And that was clearly an order.

For a game without rules, this one was managing to hedge itself in quite efficiently.

It is clear that there is a formula, but knowing it is of no help. It is quite easy to understand the chemical composition of gold, it is another to make a fortune out of it. I now had a list of ingredients, but a dash of elusive chemistry was needed to make them come alive.

In my search, I soon found myself in the company of another auntie figure, but this one had a sparkle in her eyes; she was Mary Burchell, president of the Romantic Novelists Association. She had just given a speech to their annual general meeting, a fearsome occasion for a lad all on his own. I mingled, teacup in one hand, and tried to blend in. In overheard conversation, I detected dissent from the *Woman's Weekly* Carol Smith party line. A lady of at least fifty, grey and plump, leaned over to another and said, 'I'm going to have to get into the steamy stuff, that's where the money is.' The other lady gave this the stamp of approval by bringing her rubber-tipped walking stick down heavily on the floor. And more tea flowed.

Mary Burchell's speech was listened to with great attention. After all, she has been writing romance for forty-five years. Many of the ladies in the audience were here for the same reason that I was – they too wanted to know the secret.

'I would like to think,' said Mary, 'that in a hundred years' time, someone picks up a Mary Burchell and says "Ah, this was it. Why did they never discover it in the last fifty years?" But I am bound to say I think it's extremely unlikely. But our kind of writing is read very largely by unsophisticated people, who therefore tend to have an exaggerated regard for the printed word, and that means that although we don't want to give ourselves a lot of importance, we do affect people out of all proportion to the literary worth of what we write.'

Clearly Miss Burchell lives in a real world, though you would never guess it from the titles of her books and stories: *Choose the One You'll Marry, Falsely Pledge My Love, Love Made the Choice, Then Come Kiss Me, Inherit My Heart,* and many others. Stories set backstage at grand operas are very much her trademark, and they have made her a favourite of the *Woman's Weekly* readers. She too has a formula, although like all the rest she denied its existence.

'My dear boy,' she began, 'almost every woman has had one man, not necessarily a husband, who for one moment made her feel marvellous. The whole point of writing romantic fiction is to bring back the memory of that feeling to the readers.'

I looked puzzled, and she sensed my bewilderment.

'When I started,' she told me, trying very hard to explain, 'I wrote the big scenes first and I cried over the best bits. I love to cry over the best bits of a story. You see, to me, romance is that quality which gives a certain air of respectability to our fondest dreams. Your story has got to end with a lump in the throat. That's what makes a romantic short story.'

I could see what she meant, knew what she was saying, but saw no way of applying her solution to my predicament. Then came a profound piece of advice.

'Think back,' she said, eyes sparkling, words coming crisply from her lips, 'is there any incident that you have noticed or taken part in which really moved you deeply? Did it concern a child, or an animal, a girl, an old man?'

She didn't get a reply, and probably didn't expect one; the question in itself was sufficient. She had made me realise that a romantic story comes from inside. It comes from an understanding of love and desire, of why two people are attracted. No one with a cold heart ever wrote a good romance, and if I was ever going to write one I was going to have to open my heart and put aside all thought of success bought by use of some silly notion of a formula. Very worrying.

I became the most loyal reader that a woman's magazine ever had. I would be first in the queue at the newsagent, eagerly awaiting the new issues. I could tell you which magazines came out on which day of the week and groan at the poor assistants if the *People's Friend* was late. My pockets filled with give-away lipsticks and moisturiser till I was weighed down like a shoplifter on a cheap cosmetic spree. I read, and read, and read, till I understood how each story worked; how it was constructed; how the plot was contrived to give a surprising twist, an obligatory uplift a couple of paragraphs from home. I've never been a fiction reader. Learning 'how-to' or 'why' always seemed a more valuable use of time, but now I was having to force myself into sharing the lives of heroes and heroines. Every day brought another story about a kind-hearted infant teacher who showed the path of true love to some hunk who was unhappily shackled to his advertising-executive girlfriend, who gave him champagne for tea but no real love . . .

Then there were the ones where the affair seemed

hopeless till something came to light to clear all obstacles from their way. *He* might have children but *she* didn't know that his wife was no longer living (not divorced: against the rules) and so they could be free to marry after all. Three or four times a day my spirits would rise to a crescendo of mutual bliss, an imaginary swelling of a string orchestra, an imaginary tear in the heroine's eye as '. . . and they lived happily ever after', written in stars, filled the skies. Shallow, improbable tripe. Until you sit down and try to write it.

Sitting down was the hardest bit. I had great fun talking to writers, listening to editors, smirking and mocking at magazine stories, but I was now required to produce three outlines and the fiction editor would decide which, if any, were worth pursuing. If I had a block of any kind it wasn't writer's block, it was an emotional one. The best advice so far had come from Mary Burchell, who told me to delve inside myself, drag out of my soul a moving incident. But all my instincts were against doing that, so I wrote according to what I perceived to be the formula. I wanted to write a story where the weedy little man triumphs over the flash, tough guy. I wanted an academic setting, a Brideshead feel to it. I wanted the duckling turning into a swan but, anxious to find a twist for the final paragraph, I thought I might let the hero undergo the transformation. This is the outline I wrote.

A girl works in a gymnasium. She does it merely to earn a living, although she would much rather be a writer. She loves poetry. She is invited out by one of the clients at the gym – a racing driver, a fast and lean sort of a man with a Jaguar car. The arrogant swine stands her up. When he next appears at the gym she flies into a rage and, in her anger, quotes poetry at him. A weedy little figure, wet-haired and with heavy black spectacles, absent-mindedly corrects one of her quotes. Their eyes meet. He summons up all his courage and asks her out, to a poetry lecture which he is attending. She is hardly impressed by this ordinary little chap but agrees to go, if only for the poetry. He stands her up as well. As the lights dim in the lecture theatre, he hasn't arrived. But who should appear on the stage, groomed and dressed and looking stunning – the ugly duckling who has turned into a swan of a man.

Can't you see it as a movie?

For my next story, I moved a little closer to home. I had worked for some years on a local radio station and knew what a reputation these stations had for being a hot-bed of lust and glamorous liaisons. Actually, it's not true – everyone's far too busy reading the football results or finding enough record requests to fill a ninety-minute slot to have time to get steamed up about anything else. But it seemed a good setting for a fictional romance. A hint of glamour in a mildly showbiz sort of setting and a chance to incorporate a touch of confusion which might sort itself out in the end and leave the way open for all to be happy ever after. I liked the stories with a good thread of mistaken identity running through them, and so I wove a plot around someone called Charlie . . . could be a boy, could be a girl.

Angela, a radio station engineer [good for the modern woman image, this one], sits all day gazing longingly at a disc jockey through the glass screen that divides them. They're both rather shy, and anyway each thinks the other is spoken-for because he has heard her talk of the person she lives with called Charlie – who is really a girl called Charlotte, but he doesn't know that – and Angela is always taking messages on the phone for the disc jockey from a woman called Sandy, with a rich sexy voice. In the end, they each realise the mistake the other has been making. Sandy is the DJ's agent and the voice is that of his secretary. The DJ discovers that Charlie isn't a man . . . and they all live happily ever after.

All the blood had now been squeezed from the stone. I'd got two outlines and no more. They had heroes and heroines and no bedroom stuff, but I still needed a third, a make-weight. This was difficult. I knew I was only going to have to write one of them, so why not make one story so ridiculous that the other two would shine like stars alongside it? So I dredged up a story about a dog. In truth, it was my mother-in-law's dog. An obnoxious little terrior that will raise its leg on anything that doesn't move for two minutes, including trouser legs. This creature served its first ever useful purpose by giving me my third outline.

A girl is walking along the pier with her little dog. She is trying to forget a past love. Her little dog has a habit of marking its territory, which it does on an angler who sits motionless on the pier. The man is furious. He flies into a rage and she bursts into tears and runs off. The next day she goes out, and he's fishing on the pier again. The dog starts to limp. The only quick way home is past the angler. But he turns out to be a vet, and a handsome one too . . .

Two copies were despatched. One to *Woman's Weekly* and the other to Carol Smith, who promised an agent's view.

How many romantic short-story writers have you ever heard of? I don't mean the novelists like Barbara Cartland or Jilly Cooper; their mainstream publishers ensure that their names are well displayed. I mean the ones who reap enormous rewards from women's magazines and from that oddest of publishing houses, Mills and Boon. They are to romantic fiction what Collins are to the Bible, what the *Sun* newspaper is to bosoms. They have made romance their own. But they hardly ever advertise, and never promote their writers; they don't need hype to achieve their astonishing sales figures, the envy of more literate publishing houses. Like publisher, so like writer. You'll find no Mills and Boon author 'doing a turn' on a chat show, not even a photograph on a book jacket – they are the silent greats.

I went to the best end of Southend-on-Sea to meet Violet Winspear, a romantic writer of long standing, a pillar of the Mills and Boon empire and with a bank balance to prove it. Not that you would guess that from her life-style. Her bungalow is cosy, suburban, and well furnished. The Jaguar in the drive is her brother's (it was a present from her), but nothing else is remotely flash.

It was *Woman's Weekly* who suggested Violet to me as someone from whom I might get inspiration. They had just received from her a story involving an orchestra conductor who had lost his arm in a revolving door. (This gave me an idea for a romance about a ballet dancer who loses a foot in a spin-dryer, but I suppressed it for the moment).

Violet, middle-aged, roundish and with spectacle lenses like jam jar bottoms, is an East End girl who came to fiction through telling stories to her friends. In the artificial-flower factory where she worked, long hours over the plastic tulips were passed in listening to passionate tales of romance which Violet made up as she went along. She eventually put them down on paper, and eventually wrote herself a pile of money large enough to have accountants constantly begging her to move to the Channel Islands. She always refused.

'What would I want out there?' asked Violet, bemused. 'I like it in Southend.'

There was a cosiness about her – the warmth of those who are not afraid to open their hearts, perhaps. There was a modesty too, honest disbelief that I should have come to her for advice, as if her hundred or more romances stood for nothing.

Violet breaks the rules. She has done since her very first story. It was called 'Lucifer's Angels'.

'The heroine was a divorcee,' she told me, and I drew in my breath, knowing by now what a brave departure that was.

'I regard romantic fiction as one big cake,' she went on. 'We've all got a slice and some have got a bit more spice in them than the others. I like to think my slice is a bit more interesting to crunch on.'

'Steamy, sometimes?' I suggested.

'No, not steamy. Let's say it's got a few nuts in it now and again.' She finds them all around her.

'I wander around Southend, and to me it's like a Turner landscape. I've used a lot of the seedy buildings in stories. I've moved boarding-houses to the Caribbean. There's a house I've just spotted on the seafront – I'm going to move that to Cornwall,' said with the confidence of one who has done this many times before. 'It's easy. You just make the flowers more exotic and the sun more brilliant, and you're there.'

Daring she may be (on occasions, *Woman's Weekly* have found her stories too strong), but she draws a line. 'My girls,' she told me firmly, 'don't want five minutes up against a garage door. They want more out of life than that.' But don't imagine she's a prude; this is no Cartland preaching the virtues of virginity. I asked her about 'broad, comforting shoulders', the sort of line I'd read a dozen or more times in an assortment of stories.

'Comforting is a word I would never use about a man,' she said firmly. 'You look at a man when he's stripped. He's not comforting, he's threatening. My heroines are looking for a certain amount of dominance, for sexual threat. There's nothing comforting in my heroes.' And she glanced up at the picture of Bogart on her wall.

If not comforting, how about a ruggedly handsome hero? She wasn't having any of that either.

'I wouldn't use the word handsome. Just describe him. If he's got lines on his face, say so. Tell them, he's got a craggy, lined face. He's not a smooth sort of guy.'

Heroines?

'Give her some character. Don't just say she's pretty. Make her come alive in another way. Give her an infectious laugh, a dimple in one cheek, make her eyes an odd colour. Give her a character, don't just cut her out of cardboard.'

At last, I felt I was getting the nuts and bolts of romantic fiction writing. The gimmicks. Then Violet launched herself into a long speech, straight from the heart.

'Sincerity is the key to success. It doesn't matter where the story is set as long as you get this scene going between these two people, building up to love – not just sex because, God help us, that's not the whole of life. The secret of these stories is in the loving, the knowing that somebody cares about you. We live in a society which says that if you're pretty or rich or educated you're going to get all the goodies. But your heroine isn't like that. She's not pretty, hasn't got a rich daddy, she's just an average sort of girl who finds love. It's lovely to think that you will find one person who cares so much about you. That's what we're trying to say in these stories: there *is* such a thing in this world as love.'

She convinced me. She convinces her readers and perhaps, now and again in the lonely moments over the typewriter, she believes it herself. Violet has never married.

I was dreading the verdict on my stories. There was an element of Russian roulette about it. Which of the three is loaded? Which is going to explode in my face. Which one might I get away with? I could tell from the stony look on Carol Smith's face that she was deeply unimpressed and saw no more diamond rings coming out of my little efforts.

The radio station story first.

'It's corny,' said Carol with no hesitation. 'It's so obvious that the reader is going to know in the first paragraph that it's a case of mistaken identity. Where's the drama going to come?'

In a meeting at the end where all the true identities were revealed? I suggested.

'But there isn't any story,' repeated Carol. 'It's just a situation, an anecdote that hasn't got a story. It needs a middle twist that the reader didn't foresee.'

I pre-empted her verdict. I suggested I forget the whole thing. She agreed.

I moved on to the doggy on the pier, the one that raises its leg on the angler.

Carol gave this one some careful thought.

'I like the idea of the pier, it's romantic.' My spirits lifted. 'I like the dog and the rugged bit. Angling's a good idea because it's different . . .'

Hang on Carol, this was the make-weight!

'I don't think the nice young man could be a vet, would a vet kill fish? And for God's sake find something more aesthetic for this dog to do than pee up the man's leg! Perhaps you could get a bit more drama into it. Have the dog swept off the pier in high winds and the angler dives in . . . risking his own life,' she went into a trance. 'Better still, forget the whole rotten story. Anyway, dogs peeing on people is not *Woman's Weekly*.'

One remained – the weedy guy meets the intellectual rose in the gymnasium.

'I like it, I like it, I like it. . . .' Carol was quick to react. 'Write it. WRITE IT!'

Things hadn't changed much since I was last at *Woman's Weekly*. The cupboards were still crammed with prototype stuffed toys, wafting from the kitchen down the corridor was the scent of newly invented recipes – a hundred things to do with a cup of porridge oats. And the fiction editor's desk was still piled high with manuscripts, except that this time my three outlines were on the top.

Linda looked tense.

'You have fallen into the trap, Paul,' she avoided looking me straight in the eye, 'of just using a boy-meets-girl situation. They meet, they don't know each other, in each case they have an argument. Then on the second meeting, they fall in love. And you're asking our readers to believe that? Our readers know it doesn't work like that. Let's take them one by one. The girl on the pier first . . .'

I was getting uneasy. My mind as reflected in my stories was being slowly revealed. I was being mentally undressed. I felt vulnerable.

'Do you seriously want our readers to believe that a girl is going to fall in love with a man who, in his anger, threatens to strangle her dog? I'm not even certain who the hero is. Forget that one. Let's look at the story set in the gym.'

High hopes here.

'Setting not bad,' said Linda, 'but an *awful* heroine.

You've got real problems, Paul. All your heroines are dreadful. I get the impression you don't like women very much.'

I was liking this one less and less.

'Let me quote you a bit from one of your paragraphs,' and she opened my manuscript. ' "She wasn't unattractive when she made the effort, but why bother?" That isn't our sort of heroine at all. Our heroines are people in their own right, not worried about their looks. Your heroine seems to have only one thing in mind, and that's husband-hunting.'

'Don't *Woman's Weekly* readers ever hunt husbands?' I asked cheekily.

'No. They fall in love and get married.' I was put in my place. The story I had been banking on, the one that Carol Smith with her million-dollar instinct had picked, was heading rapidly for the bin.

'Now for the one in the radio station,' said Linda, like a magistrate reading out a charge. 'If you did something with the girl, it might work. At the moment, she's bad news. Make her a more happy, more cheerful girl – maybe the sort of girl people bring their problems to. Don't have boy meets girl early on, try something round a broken relationship. There is a vague hope that it might work.'

Writers will tell you that the nastiest sight of the day is the first blank sheet of paper that goes into the typewriter. In my case it was almost as unpleasant to contemplate as my characters. Take the disc jockey in the radio station. I remembered what Violet had told me – how her best heroes were threatening, not comforting men – so on the first page I began to mould my hero: '. . . his voice betrayed not a hint of tension. Not smooth like that of a frisky young disc jockey but with a sting, a natural roughness that comes only with experience.' Then I gave him grey streaks in his black hair. That seemed to be the sort of thing they were after. He sounded terrible to me.

Then there was the heroine to deal with. *Woman's Weekly* wanted her 'assertive' but still the sort of girl you'd bring your problems to. So she got 'newly cut blonde hair' and a

'French silk scarf' to 'wrap around her nervous fingers'.
See? Sophisticated but vulnerable. But how could I make
her 'caring'? In a brilliant flash, I had the heroine meet
the hero in a supermarket where she has gone shopping on
behalf of an old lady who can't manage otherwise. Oh,
how caring.

The obvious climax to this story has to be over a
romantic dinner, hence: '*They met at eight. It was ten before
Angela felt at all relaxed . . . the murmur of intimate conversation
was music to her ears, and so was Anthony's voice. It had lost its
force and seemed to have moved deeper into his body till it was
almost a whisper . . .*'

I felt a flood of romance rising within me. The descrip-
tions poured out: '*Anthony took hold of her hand. It was a gentle
touch for a hand so broad and strong. She felt for the first time a
power, an attraction that held them together.*' My wife came in at
this point, with the news that the cat had just been sick on
the pillow again.

Linda, the fiction editor at *Woman's Weekly*, pored over
my first 4,000 words.

'It's not quite there,' she decided. 'You've given us
a good hero, with good dialogue, good plot and good
background, but you've gone and lost the heroine. Tell us
more about her – where she comes from, details like that.'
She went on, reading from what appeared to be a long list.

'Watch the hero's dialogue, he's getting a bit boyish in
places. And I *don't* think she should be longing for a kiss in
the supermarket. It's a bit too early.' I felt slightly revolted
with myself for even hinting at such promiscuity.

And so the 4,000 words became 5,000 words and I
called my work 'A Wall of Glass'. I felt I had been banging
my head against it for weeks.

Here it is. You don't have to read it all. Feel free to
skim if you like.

If wishing could have made the time go faster, then the
hands of the clock would have reached ten long ago.
The red light over the studio door would have flashed
its urgent signal and Angela's heart would beat once

more, knowing that her first programme as a producer at Centre Point Radio was at last on the air.

The waiting was the worst bit. Half a minute to go. The intercom which linked her to the programme's presenter burst into life and made her jump.

'I thought it was the stars who got the nerves, not the producers,' he said with a mischievous wink.

Even through the crackling intercom there was no hint of tension in his voice. It was as calm and reassuring as always. Not smooth like that of a joke-cracking young disc jockey but with a sting, a natural forcefulness that came only with experience. It could have been his hundredth show for Centre Point Radio, not his first.

She tried to smile back at him, but became aware that she was furiously twisting her reddish hair around her fingers, and tying knots in the end of her French silk scarf. She thought how out of place her hint of Parisian fashion would have looked in the typing pool . . .

Her mind winged back to the week before, her leaving party, and all the friends she had left behind on the secretarial floor.

'It's your last day in the pool, isn't it.' Marcus Thornhill, the station's director, had said. 'Pop upstairs for a drink before you go home, will you?'

It had seemed an innocent enough invitation and so Angela had been hardly prepared for the sight that greeted her as she knocked on his office door and walked in. The whole of Centre Point Radio was packed into Marcus' tiny office and, with typical precision, broke into 'For she's a jolly good fellow.'

'Hey, you're looking good tonight,' Alec, the radio station's engineer, had said. 'You're looking happier than I've seen you for a long time. I go for the tall, slender redheads, you know. What are you doing after the party?'

'Alec, you're an old rogue,' she'd replied with a smile that revealed a deep fondness. 'Keep your hands to yourself and pass me a drink.'

She took the first glass she was offered and sipped it hastily, more out of need than thirst.

'Mmm . . . champagne! That tasted good!'

'You deserve it, Angie, because you've worked hard for it.' It was Maggie, her boss in the typing pool. She had seen them come, and seen them go, and nothing was giving her more pleasure than Angela's promotion after five years of hard slog.

'We'll miss you down in the pool, you know,' Maggie said.

'No, you won't,' said Angela. 'By Monday I'll be just one of those wretched people upstairs.'

'Not you, Angie, not you. I've known you too long,' said Maggie. 'I've seen you give up your weekends and your evenings just to sit in those studios and learn the job. If anyone's worked harder than you to get this new job, I'd like to meet them.'

There was a loud banging. It was Marcus Thornhill trying to gain everyone's attention with the heavy use of an inkpot and little regard for the polish on his desk.

'I'm going to make a short speech – ' there was a loud cheer – 'just to say I know that Angela is going to be missed by you all, but your loss is our listeners' gain.'

There was a huge cheer and a small parcel was thrust into Angela's hand.

'Open it up,' said Maggie. 'It's from all of us.'

Angela carefully removed the paper and felt the touch of the leather before she had a chance to realise what it was.

'It feels beautiful, whatever it is,' she said. The paper fell away.

'Oh, it's perfect. My favourite poems . . . It's just what I need for my collection. Thank you all very much!' she tried to shout above the noise of the resumed chatter.

'Open it up,' said Maggie.

Angela turned the pages, and read the inscription.

'*To a great friend, with many thanks from your mates.*' She could have cried.

'Can you step outside a minute.' It was Marcus.

They closed the door behind them, although the buzz from the party still made it difficult to hold a conversation.

'It's about your new job,' he said, dropping his voice a tone.

'I knew it was all a dream,' said Angela. 'Are you telling me it's off?'

'Not quite. But I've got a problem,' he explained. 'One of my regular producers has asked me if he can take a few days off, some kind of family trouble. I wonder if you'd like to fill in?'

'Of course, I'd love to. In at the deep end, eh?' said Angela.

'Before you say yes,' said Marcus, 'you ought to know that it's the new Anthony Ingrams show I'm asking you to produce. It's his first show for us and it's very important to the station. He's a tough man but I think you can do it . . . You can say no if you like. I won't hold it against you.'

The ticking of the clock brought her back to the present. The sweeping hand moved towards ten.

'I must have been mad ever to have wanted to do a job like this,' she muttered in a rare moment of self-doubt. As she said the words, she glanced at the switches to check that Anthony Ingrams could not hear her through the wall of glass between them. Angela Faber was too much of a perfectionist to put her fears on public display.

Anthony Ingrams, award-winning reporter and radio Journalist of the Year at only twenty-nine, and now hired by Centre Point Radio to turn its audience of thousands into millions, had style. It wasn't just his looks, although he did have that slight hint of a tan which comes after a summer spent on America's West Coast, even if he did claim he'd spent most of his holiday sweating beneath television studio lights.

Perhaps it was his sparkling blue eyes, his athletic

poise, his devastating smile that made her mutter now, 'This man has got style.'

'Thank you very much. I thought you'd never notice . . .' She spun in her chair, fearing that this time Ingrams really had heard her murmurings. But it was only Alec. Alec, the rock on which Centre Point Radio was built. As a station engineer, his technical abilities were never in doubt and neither was his good humour nor his willingness to be the butt of everyone's joke. His pear-shaped, cardigan-clad frame seemed to absorb it all, together with large quantities of strong sweet tea from a pint-sized, chipped mug which was never more than a few inches from his reach.

'No, I was referring to him.' She pointed at the figure on the other side of the glass wall. 'Don't look so hurt,' she added.

To hurt Alec would be the last thing that Angela would wish to do. Over endless glasses of beer, she had listened to his tales of loves that never were. Alec asked no more of her than that she should listen, and by listening, and helping, she had developed a great fondness for him.

He took a deep breath.

'We'll see exactly what this Ingrams fellow has got going for him. Hang on to your hats!' he muttered, and announced, 'Ten seconds to go,' as his finger-tips fell on to the faders and the red light came to life.

'Good day to you. This is Centre Point Radio. My name is Anthony Ingrams and the issues of the day are my concern. You can call me on . . .'

The needles flickered to the rhythm of his voice, the clock moved on, and Angela sighed with relief. She had waited so long for this day to come . . .

'Many are called, but few are ever chosen,' were Marcus Thornhill's words the first time he had refused to give her a job. She remembered how it had made her more determined to do what she knew she could do well – make radio shows.

Her life-long friend and flatmate, Charlie, had been a great help to her over the difficult patches when ambition could so easily have given way to uncertainties. She had been a close friend since schooldays. Then, she had called herself by her real name, Charlotte, but 'Charlie', she thought, looked better on the gossip pages, and the name stuck. It was a wise choice, given that Charlie was unlikely to excel at anything other than attracting publicity helped by her family background, her looks, and her talent for capturing the attentions of the most eligible men in town.

Charlie's path through life had not been entirely smooth, and when her world was about to shatter, it was Angela who was at the ready to hold it together.

As a flatmate, Charlie had infuriating habits. Like disappearing without paying her half of the bills, or leaving Angela to deal with a queue of suitors who came calling, only to find that Charlie had flown. But the art of the doorstep brush-off was good practice, Angela decided, for the day when she would have to turn away politicians and self-publicists, all fighting for air time on the Anthony Ingrams show.

She dragged her thoughts back to the present again . . . Ingrams was giving a first-class performance. He dismissed a self-seeking local councillor with a few crisp questions and was now steaming through the phone-in part of his show.

Angela worked flat-out, checking the callers, keeping an eye on the clock, the commercials and the newsbreaks. It had been a great compliment to be allowed to work on this show, and she wasn't going to let down those who had faith in her. But she had no doubts that it was really Anthony Ingrams in charge. The ridiculous he despatched with a sharp remark, while the uncertain were made to feel confident.

He had a remarkable way with old people. He listened for five patient minutes while a housebound old lady told him how her home had now become a prison.

The news bulletin gave them all a chance to breathe.

Angela turned to Alec who had been hanging on to every one of Ingrams' words – a rare compliment.

'See what I mean? He's got style, and he's tough,' said Angela. Alec took a pause.

'Yeah, he's tough all right, but not nasty with it, know what I mean?'

She nodded, and as she did so, the intercom burst into life.

'Get the phone number of that old lady, will you?' said Ingrams, crisply, in between sips of water. Angela scribbled the number on to a slip of paper and took it into the studio. She watched him fold it and put it into his inside pocket and she guessed what it was for.

'I imagine you'll want to feature her in your newspaper column?'

Ingrams dropped his voice.

'Something like that,' he replied and went on scribbling notes.

The show was going well but Angela was doubtful about Ingrams' next guest interview and she felt now was the time to voice her doubts.

'I'm worried about Lord Reendale,' she said. 'Are you sure he's the right man for a discussion on industrial development in the City?'

It was a brave thing to ask, since Ingrams had made it clear that this was far from being the first time he had interviewed Lord Reendale, and always with great success.

'What makes you think he might not be the right man?' asked Ingrams.

'It was just something in his voice,' said Angela, trying to crystallise the nagging doubt in her mind. 'He just sounded a bit surprised that I should be asking him.'

'I think it was probably his telephone manner,' said Ingrams. 'I'm sure everything will be fine. He was on one of my other shows a year or two ago.'

Just as Angela was about to return to her seat in the control room, the studio door opened.

'I'm looking for the Anthony Ingrams show . . .' said the young man, dressed in a blazer, white shirt and polished black shoes, the whole effect being spoilt only by his faded jeans.

Ingrams rose to his full six feet, looked down at the young man and said, smiling, 'I *am* the Anthony Ingrams show. Can I help you?'

'Er, I'm Peter . . .' said the young man, almost apologising.

'Reendale,' said Angela, finishing the sentence for him, suddenly recognising the crisp public school voice from their brief telephone conversation that morning.

Ingrams slipped into his chair.

'I think you interviewed my father,' said the young man, 'not long before his death.'

Ingrams' mind was working at full stretch. Before him *was* Lord Reendale – but not the Lord Reendale he had been expecting. He must have been out of the country when the father had died.

He showed the young man to his seat on the other side of the microphone while Angela dived for the control room and the row of books along the back shelf.

'We're in for some fireworks now,' said Alec, who had heard the conversation through his headphones. 'I'll bet that young lad knows less about industrial development than I do. We'll see how much style this Ingrams fellow has got now,' and he took a gulp of his stewed tea as if to steady himself for the storm he felt was about to break.

Angela grabbed the thickly bound copy of *Who's Who*, sensing, as Alec had done, that a mighty disaster was about to strike. Her finger ran down the page. The newsbreak was nearly over as her eyes arrived at Lord Reendale's entry:

REENDALE Bt Peter b. 1953

> *Chairman, Council*
> *for Youth Activities . . .*

She heard the final words of the news bulletin and saw Ingrams' finger move towards his microphone switch. She threw herself at the intercom and whispered, 'Forget the discussion on industry, try youth unemployment!'

Ingrams nodded, grudgingly, and waited till the final notes of the news jingle had died away.

'. . . and with me this morning is Lord Reendale who is, of course, well known for his work amongst young people in the City . . .'

'Well done, love, that's the way to do it,' said Alec, being unusually free with his compliments.

She allowed herself a moment of self-congratulation.

The two-hour show passed more quickly than Angela would have thought possible, and as the signature tune died away Ingrams straightened his tie and marched out of the studio.

'I signed up with this radio station expecting to work with professionals, not raw beginners. May I suggest, young lady – ' fixing Angela with his piercing blue eyes – 'that you are a little more careful who you invite on to my show in the future?'

The door slammed behind him and if Angela hadn't known that her instinct had been right, and he had been wrong, she would have felt crushed.

She moved quickly towards the door, her face flushed with anger. 'I'm going to tell that big-head exactly what I think of him . . . and they can sack me if they like.'

And she would probably have done so if Alec hadn't persuaded her that answering the insistent phone was more important.

It was a call for Ingrams.

'Hi, have I missed Tony?' She had never heard anyone call him Tony before. It was a smooth voice, a young, silky voice belonging to a woman who clearly knew Anthony well.

'I'm afraid he's left. Can I take a message or have him call you back?' she said, reverting into her secretarial clear-headedness.

'Would you tell him I loved the show? Tell him Sandie called.'

She didn't bother to make a note of the name, or write down the message. She felt it was a voice she couldn't easily forget.

She little expected to bump into Ingrams in the supermarket, even if it was next door to the radio station. If they hadn't both reached for the same packet of sugar, she might not have spotted him since she was still reeling from the events of the morning, and Ingrams was clearly steering a trolley for the first time in his life and it was demanding his whole concentration.

'I'm very sorry, Angela. I think I ought to apologise,' he said.

'There's no need to,' she said, summoning all her resolution to look him calmly in the eye as she did so. 'I'll have the next packet, they're all the same.'

'Not the sugar.' He smiled. 'About this morning. You were right about young Lord Reendale and I was wrong. You saved the show. It never crossed my mind that the old boy would have died. I'm very sorry. Look, I'd feel much better if you'd let me buy you dinner . . . tonight.'

'I'd love to,' she said, dropping her packet of sugar into his trolley.

They met at eight. It was ten before Angela felt at all relaxed. The beef had been deliciously rare, the wine smooth, and the distant chink of glasses and the murmur of intimate conversation was becoming music to her ears.

And so was Anthony's voice. It had lost its force. It was softer and seemed to have moved deeper within him.

'You can call me Tony if you like,' he told her and poured her another glass of the richly red wine.

Her eyes widened in horror. 'Oh, dear, I quite forgot. There was a call for you this morning. It was someone called Sandie who said to tell you the show was great.'

Ingrams smiled.

'Ah, Sandie, now there's a friend if ever I needed one. When you've spent as much time with your nose deep in your work as I have, you suddenly look up and wonder where all your old mates went. But Sandie's always there, always ready to listen. I might look tough as rock, but I need to talk sometimes . . . like I'm talking to you.'

It was quite a speech. Angela felt she had to say something, though she feared the answer to the only question she really wanted to ask.

'You and Sandie must be very good friends.'

He nodded.

'We can talk for hours, just like this. You know, in an odd sort of way, you remind me a lot of Sandie.'

But the compliment was lost on Angela. She remembered only that cool, silky voice on the telephone and wondered why she hated it so much.

'Do you have anyone you can talk to, Angela?' said Anthony.

'Not really,' said Angela, somewhat surprised by his question.

'You'll forgive my asking, but I overheard you on the phone to Charlie the other day. Is Charlie a close . . . ?'

But before he could finish, Angela glanced at her watch.

'It's half-past eleven. I really must go,' she said, wishing to bring the conversation to a halt and, with it, any mention of Sandie.

'Is it that late?' cried Ingrams, fumbling for cash to pay the bill. 'And I promised the old lady I'd . . .'

'Promised what old lady what?' said Angela.

'I promised to take some shopping round to that old lady who was on the phone-in this morning,' he said, 'but it's too late now.'

Angela remembered what she had said in the studio that morning; how she had assumed Anthony had wanted the old lady's phone number so he could write her into yet another story. How wrong she'd been!

It was a rare glimpse into the private life of Anthony Ingrams, a side of his character she would never have guessed existed. Here was a man whose hard, professional exterior hid a genuinely warm heart.

For the first time since she had known him, he looked bewildered, a little lost. She felt an urge to help him.

'I'll take the shopping round tomorrow morning,' she said.

'Thanks,' he said simply and took hold of her hand. It was a gentle touch for a hand so broad and strong. She felt, for the first time, a power, an attraction that held them together.

For Angela, their touch was all too brief.

As he smiled, his face seemed to relax.

'I've enjoyed tonight,' he said. 'Let's have lunch next week. Sandie's coming up for the day. We'll all go out together.'

Her beautiful moment was shattered by the mention of Sandie's name. She wanted to say no. She didn't want to meet this satin-voiced girl. But she couldn't refuse. She drove off into the night, wondering whether Sandie cared as much for Anthony as she now knew she did.

With every lunchtime phone call that Sandie made, Angela grew more convinced there was no place in Anthony's life for her. The wall of glass between them grew thicker, more impenetrable as the days went by . . . till Thursday came.

Angela had woken feeling happy with the world, and it was a few minutes before her peace of mind was shattered by thoughts of the lunchtime meeting with Sandie. Things might have been easier if the first thing she came across as she stumbled into the kitchen hadn't been a hastily scribbled note from Charlie.

'*Darling Angie,*

Popping over to France for a few days with Roger. Haven't got a penny on me. Will settle with you when I get back.

Love, Charlie.

PS If Philip calls, tell him I'm away and you don't know when I'll be back.'

Angela's temper was already short.

'I think Charlie can do me a favour for a change,' she muttered, stuffing a slice of bread into the toaster.

She swept into Charlie's room, opened the wardrobe door and took a long, hard look. 'I don't see why I shouldn't be the height of fashion for just one day,' she said as she reached for a dress.

Slightly understated, she thought, but distinctly stylish, and very fashionable. It fitted like a dream, but there again, Angela and Charlie had swapped clothes since school days so it came as no surprise. It was a simple dress, made of wool and enhanced the green in her eyes.

'Thank you, Charlie,' she said as she looked in the mirror. 'Let's call it your half of the gas bill, shall we?'

'Morning, Angela.' It was Alec. 'You look a million dollars. Are you sure you're not doing anything tonight?'

'Not now, Alec,' said Angela, turning away, and Alec continued on his way into the studio.

Ingrams was sitting there, stop watch in one hand, a copy of *The Times* in the other. 'Angela looks a bit glum,' he said. 'What's wrong with her, Alec?'

'I suppose it's the usual old problem. It's probably Charlie giving her a bad time. She'll soon get over it.'

'She's a nice girl, Alec,' said Ingrams. 'What kind of a guy is this Charlie to give her a bad time?'

But there was no reply. Alec's headphones were clasped firmly to his head and his attention was taken by his mug of tea which was in grave danger of growing cold if urgent steps weren't taken.

The red light went off at midday and Ingrams rushed out of the studio.

'Is Sandie here yet?' he asked with an impatience that Angela tried not to find hurtful. Before she had time to answer, he was through the door and she could hear his footsteps quicken as he raced to the reception desk.

She opened the door and followed, breathing more

1a. At the Waterside Inn with Michel Roux

1b.
With teammate Mark,
agonising over the *agneaux*

2a. Early training days – John Parker at his most worried

2b. The Duke of Edinburgh points out the intricacies of dressage

3a. 'First' – after presentation and dressage

3b. Bollio and Agy plunge bravely through the water hazard

4a. Terry Scott warns me:
'You say, I'll go and sweep the roads, but let me out of this
agony'

4b. Marti Caine gives Ada the northern touch

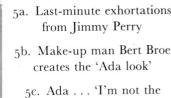

5a. Last-minute exhortations from Jimmy Perry

5b. Make-up man Bert Broe creates the 'Ada look'

5c. Ada ... 'I'm not the woman I appear to be'

6a. A friendly lick from Tim

6b. One man, his dog and a flock of stroppy sheep

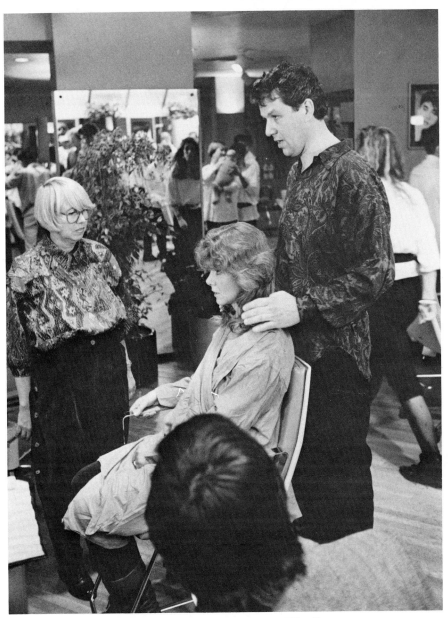

7. A nerve-wracking moment for Jilly Cooper,
just before the first cut

8a. Kessler, trying to 'think like a mugger,
a man who would barbecue his own granny'

8b. Michael Caine gasps at my bravura performance

deeply now, and forced a smile before turning into the reception area.

'Sandie, long time no see. How are you?' she heard him say as she turned the corner, unprepared for a shock that took her breath away.

Before her stood Anthony, shaking the hand of a tall young man with long, straight black hair, horn-rimmed glasses and an engaging smile. Beside him stood the smartest leather briefcase she had ever seen.

'Angela, I'd like you to meet my agent, Sandie. He's been a good pal over the years.'

Her lips moved but she could find no words. Sandie strode across to her. 'Hello, Angela. Tony's told me so much about you.'

She took his hand.

'And this is Janice, my secretary,' added Sandie as a willowy blonde stepped forward.

'I think you two have spoken on the phone,' he added.

Janice said hello in that cool, silky voice that Angela had grown to dislike so much. She had been right to have placed it with such an attractive girl, for Janice could indeed have stepped down from a pin-up calendar. Angela's only mistake was to assume it was Sandie to whom she had been speaking.

She looked first at Anthony and then Sandie. She could see why Anthony liked him so much. He had a nice smile, a sparkle in his eye. An easy man to share your troubles with.

Angela could almost have laughed when she realised how stupid she had been.

And then a piercing scream cut through the air.

'Darling, that's where my dress is! My flight was delayed so I came home for some . . .' It was Charlie, firing on all cylinders.

Alec appeared, and filled what little space was left in the now crowded reception.

'What in heaven's name is going on?' he asked.

'I'd like to know what's going on too,' muttered Anthony.

'Anthony, this is my friend Charlie – and I'm wearing her half of the gas bill,' said Angela with just a hint of hysteria creeping into her voice.

'You're all going mad,' said Anthony. Charlie looked across at him and, realising she was in the company of a personality, swept round the room to introduce herself.

Some time later, when everyone's attention was engaged, Anthony led Angela round the corner, out of sight of the growing crowd.

He placed both his hands firmly on her shoulders.

'It's time we talked,' he said, pulling her towards him till she could feel the warmth of his body. She felt slightly threatened by his sudden display of force which within a moment turned into the most gentle of touches. She had no power to resist.

'Why didn't you tell me Charlie was your flatmate?' his voice was once again deep and soft. She looked into his blue eyes. She was a million miles away from Centre Point Radio.

He continued. 'If I hadn't thought Charlie was some boy friend of yours, I might have told you long ago that I loved you.'

He released his grip for a moment to give her a chance to move away, but she only edged closer to him.

'I do love you, Angela. I've watched you through the glass, your hair, your smile, the warmth in your eyes. I feel I know you so well, and yet I'm holding you for the first time . . . now there's no Charlie to . . .' His voice faded away, drowned in the intensity of their embrace.

She wanted to say how much she loved him. How much she had wanted him, how much she had longed to hear the very words he had just spoken, but she could find no words. She took hold of his hands and pressed them to her to remind her that this was really happening.

Charlie's voice came flashing through the air like a rocket.

'We're going to lunch together, aren't we, Sandie

darling?' and before Sandie had time to protest, they were out of the door.

'She's a fast worker,' said Anthony, not allowing his eyes to move for one second from Angela's.

'I'm afraid I know that tone in her voice,' said Angela. 'I hope Sandie can look after himself.'

'He can cope,' said Anthony. 'It's me I'm worried about. You can't think much of a man who has spent sleepless nights worrying over a girl's boy friend who doesn't even exist.'

She rested her head on his chest.

'It's the sort of mistake anyone could have made,' she said, and knowing that her face was buried deep in his shoulder, she allowed herself a smile as his arms moved around her and pressed her closer.

After a long moment, he relaxed his grip and tilted her chin so he could gaze into her eyes.

'Darling . . .' she murmured, feeling ridiculously shaky under that intense look. 'Oh, darling Tony . . .'

But the rest was lost as he bent his head to kiss her once more.

Peace had settled on Centre Point Radio. Alec looked around the reception area. Sandie and Charlie were at lunch. He couldn't work out where Angela and Anthony were. There was only him and Janice left.

'Fancy a mug of tea, luv?' said Alec hopefully.

THE END

There was not what you might call a spontaneous outburst of praise, or of anything for that matter. No million-dollar phone calls from Carol Smith – indeed, I had to phone her. It was a rather serious matter. It had been brought to my attention that *Woman's Weekly* expected *women* writers. Even if they were men, they had to have women's names. What was mine to be, I asked Carol.

'Your name should be romantic,' she paused to choose her words, 'but with a touch of steel.'

I took her at her word.

'Paula Steele,' I told *Woman's Weekly*; they hastily accepted.

The only other change they made was that when my story was eventually published the front cover of the magazine had been altered. Where it usually proclaimed 'Famed for its Fiction', that particular week's issue read 'Famed for its Knitting'.

Clubbed
to
Death

Clubbed to Death

What makes comics such sad men – even cheery Ken Dodd or laugh-a-minute Les Dawson? There's sadness in Marti Caine and Terry Scott too – for backstage you'll see comedians stripped of their gags and left with nothing but a head full of doubts, their minds weighed down with insecurity, their faces drawn and glum. It's always a shock to meet a comic off-stage. But why should it be? You don't expect to meet Olivier in the street and find him intoning Shakespeare, or bump into Val Doonican humming the 'Londonderry Air'. We seem to expect more of comics, because they have the power to reduce us to that state of uninhibited relaxation where we can laugh out loud: a power over us which we can enjoy but will never understand.

Comics don't always understand the chemistry either, and I suspect that is the root of many of the doubts that can suffocate them. They don't know why we think they are funny, and because they have no control over the secret of their success how can they be sure that it is not draining away? That's why they relentlessly put themselves to the test, and why they are sad men. For to go out on stage and be unfunny is the cruellest and most crushing of experiences. I speak as one who knows – I tried to be a stand-up comic and failed horribly.

As one comic warned me, 'Being a comic is like going into a bull-ring. Your blood turns to ice. In your case, Paul, it's like giving you half a dozen riding lessons and putting you in the Grand National.'

I think the whole episode is best examined as if it were a tragic accident; to discover its cause, you must first turn over the wreckage. So come to the Lakeside Club, Frimley

Green: a nightclub set amidst the half-timbered wastes of Surrey, scene of my comic début. (The omens were never good. On my way there, my taxi driver stopped a nurse to ask the way. 'You'd better ask in casualty,' she replied.)

It is late one March evening. I have just come off stage to applause. Polite rather than tumultuous.

'You're lucky – they didn't throw things!' some wag offers.

At least it would have been a reaction. I have just stood on that stage for ten very long minutes, armed with fifty or more gags constructed by a top scriptwriter and advice from some of the best comics in the land, but still the audience did not laugh at me. They didn't even find the clothes funny. I did it in drag, but I was no tarty Danny La Rue – more a cuddly Blackpool landlady figure. And what a figure! Padded boobs like barrage balloons, ginger hair like wire wool, an apron twice its natural weight through added gravy stains, pink pom-pom slippers and a bright blue cardigan hand-knitted by somebody with a twitch. But they didn't seem to find that lot funny either.

It has been the longest ten minutes of my life. Minute after minute of talking to a wall; joke after joke falling dead like elastic that has lost its stretch. Gem after gem cast, like pearls, before this herd of swine. This is the comic's nightmare; when he wakes up in the night, dripping in sweat, turning and writhing, it is this he is dreaming of. It is the unmistakable emanation of a thousand blank and unmoved faces. Even if the ground were to open under you and you were to disappear, even that would be no relief; the wounds go deep and the scars will stay.

Who was I to blame? Who caused this dreadful, mutilating accident? As I say, let us turn over the wreckage.

It would be very easy to blame Jimmy Perry, an obvious scapegoat if ever there was one. He wrote the script, penned the song at the end of the routine, taught me the moves – 'created' me, if you like. If the cake turns out rotten you blame the cook, but can I really blame Jimmy for any of this?

He is a man of enormous reputation. He has co-written some of the finest television comedy of the last fifteen years – *Dad's Army* and *Hi-De-Hi*, for example, are Jimmy's creations. So he knows something about TV gags, anyway. But he was not born of a television background: he's been an actor-manager and a comic, he was in panto and in farce. His life is steeped in show business of every sort.

You'd never catch him wearing the same suit twice; I counted over a dozen in our short acquaintance, each with matching glasses. He'll tell you how he had his teeth fixed, too, ('I'm very into teeth'). He's one of the old school who has found fame and fortune in the new age, but not public recognition. Jimmy would love to be a TV face instead of a TV credit name.

'I went to Arthur Lowe's funeral,' he told me, 'and the photographers thought it would be nice to have a picture of the Dad's Army crowd. We all got into line and he told me to clear off. He said what had I got to do with it?'

'We've got to think of a name for you that sounds funny,' said Jimmy, commencing his latest character creation. 'Some names are funny, some aren't. Take Gorgonzola – that's funny, Cheddar isn't. So what do you think? How about *Ada*, that's a funny name.'

Ada it was.

'The first thing you've got to do, Paul,' he said as he revealed these tablets of theatrical wisdom, 'is to find a North Country housewife to base Ada on.'

That was no problem. I'd spent a South Yorkshire childhood in the clutches of these vast-bosomed ladies. For many years I believed all women had nothing in their mouths but gums, that curlers grew in their hair and that they all lived in a state of petty dispute with the next-door neighbour. I remember that when they kissed you, they left dripping wet pools on your cheeks. One lady whose memory still haunts me had a remarkable ability to expel tomato seeds whilst speaking, many hours after finishing a juicy sandwich.

No problems visualising the character, Jimmy.

'I don't write jokes,' declared Jimmy. 'When I write,

the lines are coming from the characters, so I'm not going to give you a list of gags to do. I'm going to write a story for you to tell with funny lines in it.'

I could see what he meant; it's what all my comic heroes do. Victor Borge never tells gags – it's a narrated wander through his mind – and George Burns did the same.

'If you're telling a story, they'll listen,' said Jimmy.

Getting an audience to listen, however, is not the full measure of my task. Judges get attentive audiences when passing sentence, but not many laughs.

'I'll make certain you get a few laughs to start off with,' promised Jimmy, as if it were as easy as flicking a switch, 'and once you've got the first it will be marvellous. You'll be away.'

With my confidence inflated by that promise, I floated away and awaited the script. It is far too easy to get carried away by showbiz chat. 'Darling, you're going to be wonderful,' works well for those who are wonderful already and aren't harmed by an occasional reminder. But if you've never in your life been before an audience with the intention of making them laugh, to be told you will be 'certain to get a few laughs to start off with' is like telling a first-time wire-walker that no one ever falls off: you can't make promises like that, and only fools believe them. So if I made an early mistake, it was in believing that all this was achievable. I assumed there was no more to baking this cake than putting all the ingredients together and giving them a good mix.

How do you tell a joke? What's the magic something that goes into a few lines of story-telling that makes it funny from one man's lips and desperately dull from another's?

Of the ones who *can't* tell jokes well, there are two groups: the ones who begin, 'stop me if you've heard this one,' signalling instantly their lack of confidence that people will laugh. Then there are those who wait till they're in a crowded bar, ten minutes short of closing time, where the poorest of gags gets a raucous reception.

These are the dangerous ones – they really think they're funny.

I'm neither; I'm not a joke-teller at all. If I am even tempted, I hear myself beginning to sound like the closing-time gagster, or folding up like the apologist, and I cringe inside and give up the idea.

I know that timing is the secret. I know that a good comic can have his audience writhing with laughter without saying a word. He can create such an expectation in their mind that when the punchline fails to materialise, the look on his face alone can make them dissolve into laughter. Then there's Ken Dodd's technique of machine-gunning gags at an audience, another kind of timing. Jimmy was going to have to determine which technique would work for me.

But first the script. Comedy scripts always look rather poor to me. Fireworks would be dull if you could squeeze the 'whoosh' back into the tube and watch it again and see how it worked, so jokes on paper have never made me laugh – not even the published Hancock or *Yes, Minister* scripts. And Jimmy's script didn't either. It was an 'over the bosom' monologue by the old bag we had decided to call Ada; it was spat out rather than delivered, and across an ironing board. In it she tells us of her unhappy relationship with her much-loathed neighbours. It is a tale of human contempt; there is such a tale down every street, and there has been as long as there have ever been neighbours. As comics say, 'the old ones are the best'.

'She's got so many double chins, she looks as though she's peering at you over the top of a pile of pancakes.'

That's the first joke, and it sets the tone of the script. I don't know how *you* would tell that, but I thought I might try it with a hint of rising incredulity in the voice; a touch of the 'you won't believe this but . . .' about it. Remember too the bosom-heaving that might accompany it. So that's the way I did it for Jimmy at our first rehearsal, arms crossed as if supporting the barrage balloons.

'No, no,' said Jimmy, 'you're not seeing the picture. You're not understanding it. Structure it. Do it step by step. Build it up. She's got . . . so many chins . . . (now lift your voice a bit) . . . she looks (up further) as though she's peering at you over . . . (build to climax) the top of a pile of pancakes. Build it all the time.'

So I tried the next gag.

'She never gives him a minute's peace. What with her nagging him on one side and her mother nagging him on the other side, he's the only man down our street who gets nagged in stereo.'

I read. I built it up, like the pile of pancakes.

'You won't get a laugh like that,' scolded Jimmy, 'you've got to paint a picture. Imagine him being nagged on one side, then on the other side – you must paint the picture as you tell the joke. What I've given you here is character comedy – the laughs come from the picture you create. I've put about twenty sure-fire gags into the script, but there'll still be huge chunks where you might not get a laugh. But that will be all right because they'll be listening and thinking of the picture that you're painting. It's actually a bit more difficult than giving you a string of gags. I'm taking a bit of a risk by giving you this.'

Who did you say was taking the risk, Jimmy?

I had to learn the script off by heart. It seemed endless, and, being a reporter rather than an actor, I found that other people's words didn't come easily. When your natural habit is to dig the words from the inside of your own head, it isn't easy to reverse the process and stuff other people's in there, especially Jimmy's. My lips were never still for the next few weeks. I couldn't learn the lines by going over them in my head, I had to speak them. On trains I could only mutter, but in parks I could do it out loud. In parks I also felt free to do the actions as well, so I would be striding along, heaving my imagined bosom and doing all the actions of a fifteen-stone Blackpool landlady – but dressed in overcoat and trousers. People kept their distance and mothers hurriedly pushed their children out of my path but, oblivious, I would stride on, heaving and pouting, occasionally delving into my overcoat pocket for a crumpled piece of paper with the script on it. Thousands of fellow train-travellers, countless innocent walkers and shoppers were now sharing my routine.

In a profession where the secret of success is intangible, you couldn't blame a comic if he wanted to keep what understanding he has of his craft to himself. Why should any comic tell you how he gets an audience to laugh for him? – it could be it's you they're laughing for tomorrow, instead of him. But I didn't come across any sense of rivalry. Either because they didn't see me as a threat or, more likely, because comics feel a bit like soldiers going into battle; if a new recruit has the guts to go and fight the battle, he's got a right to be told how to fire the guns.

That's how Beryl Reid and I came to be hobbling across a carpet looking like a pair of arthritics trying to do the 'Military Two-Step'.

Tiny Beryl Reid, less than chest height on me. She beams, she radiates warmth and kindness and an honest desire to help in any way she can. She's a comic actress rather than a comic, but it wasn't her humour I was trying to tap; it was her techniques of characterisation, the way she assumes the guise of cheery old ladies and dotty old bats.

'Do you feel like a big Ada?' she asked in a pointed sort of way. 'You have to feel like that woman. What would she wear on her feet? Think first of how she would walk.'

Beryl's eyes sparkled. It was like playing charades with a favourite old aunt. We both took our shoes off.

'She'd be very flat-footed because she's carried a lot of parcels.' Beryl was right. All those fat old ladies of my childhood put one flat foot in front of the other as they shuffled along, burdened down by bags of shopping and brown paper carriers full of washing.

'I think she'd probably have fluffy slippers because she sees herself as a bit of a sex symbol.'

Beryl staggered across the room humping her imaginary shopping. Perfect. She aged thirty years in as many seconds. Now my turn. Not so easy.

'Just pretend you're very old suddenly . . . start shuffl-ing. I can't hear your feet shuffle.' It's very easy to concentrate too hard, as I was doing. She'd already told me the secret – just think old – but it's easier said than done.

'Your body's too straight. Your bottom's gone in but your back should be a bit more rounded . . . it's coming . . . it's coming,' she said kindly.

Of course, it wasn't. All I was doing was beginning to feel a bit of an Ada, but in the wrong way.

'Just think of your feet,' she urged me again, 'and it will all come to you.' The frustration of trying to understand, of reaching out for this straw and knowing that half the battle would be over if I could just grasp it, became unbearable. It's like learning to tie a new knot – easy to watch and comprehend, but impossible to repeat.

The more frustrated I became, the further I got from the character. If I could just 'think myself old' all the rest would follow, but this was still an enormous stride to take. I shuffled back across the room, trying hard to remember if the shoulders went back, or was it the tummy that went in? Exactly the wrong approach. If you think old, and become old, you'd know if your shoulders were rounded enough. Poor old Beryl watched all this with the perpetual smile of an Auntie who only wanted to encourage, and gave me a goodbye kiss to send me on my way.

I decided to take a straw poll, a sort of clutching-at-a-straw poll. I wanted to know from the comic giants what made them tick; why did they get the laughs, what can I do to get the laughs?

Ken Dodd first. To his public he's hair and teeth, Diddy Men and tickling sticks, but he's a technician; he can tell you how one joke works in Huddersfield but the same gag dies a death in Glasgow – he's a joke doctor. I submitted myself and a variety of gags for examination.

Telling a gag to a comic calls for nerve, especially ones about boarding-house landladies.

'I rang the doorbell. This woman answered. She said, "Do you want a five-pound room or a six-pound room?" I said, "What's the difference?" She said, "The six-pound room's got a bed in it!"'

Dodd was unmoved, except for his mouth which fell open.

'With that sort of joke,' he said, 'don't try a club. You'd be better off at a church hall, or perhaps a harvest supper.' He paused a comic's pause of exactly the right length. 'I wouldn't have done that at all,' he added, 'I would have said: I knocked on the door and this lady said, "What do you want?" [voice raised to scraggy falsetto] I said, "Do you think the lady next door will give me a glass of water?"'

It worked. It was funny. I couldn't tell you why.

'You've got to make yourself into a character, into a person they're either going to have sympathy with or they're going to admire. I think you've got to go out and observe. Watch how the ladies behave. Get some good gags and observe.' And then the advice that perhaps I should have taken, but didn't: 'Get hold of this Perrier water man, Perry or whatever his name is, and tell him to come up with some new stuff!'

Why didn't I do just that? Dodd himself provided the answer. *He'd* taken one of Jimmy's jokes, done it his way and made it work. That's the skill I thought I was looking for – turning words on paper into solid laughs, not new gags.

Jimmy didn't like my tour of the stars. He accused them all of having too much 'self-interest', but I found exactly the reverse. They were all too concerned for my welfare. At some time or other in their successful careers they had been through the ordeal that faced me and they wanted to ease the path in any way they could. I went to see Terry Scott because of his reputation for having mastered the panto dame, exactly the role I was trying to achieve, and he boosted my confidence in Jimmy's material.

'If you haven't got confidence when you walk out on the stage,' Scott warned, 'the audience will smell it. You may be going on with the corniest joke in the world but if you tell it with confidence, someone will laugh.'

And where does that confidence come from?

'You have to say to yourself, it doesn't matter who is

top of the bill, it's *me* they've all come to see. That gives
me the confidence to go on. But you must do the lines that
make you laugh. Even if a top writer has given you a good
line, if you don't like it, don't do it.'

The recipes for success had come thick and fast. Confidence, belief, will – all these notions were thrust at me.
Only Scott warned me of the price of failure, of the horror
of the performance that fails, and he chose his words
carefully.

'You say, I'm sorry I even thought I could do it. I'll go
and sweep the roads, but let me out of this agony.'

One more comic, one more sad man.

But there was nothing sad about me at this stage. I'd
heard Jimmy's jokes on the lips of a top comic or two and
they had made me laugh – there was nothing wrong with
the script. What's more, I knew it off by heart. I'd worked
out one or two movements and a few significant points at
which to twang my bra straps, which Jimmy thought
would get a laugh. Then there was the ironing board.
Jimmy suggested I had a quick spit on the iron now and
again, and get another laugh.

So, on the outside, I was fine. Clothes were perfect:
baggy and slightly mucky with the most severe mismatch
of colours imaginable. I was beginning to smell the fried
fish on them and see the dried tomato seeds sticking to the
cardigan. The wig helped too – long, flowing locks of filthy
ginger hair, matted like the coat of a shaggy dog that
hadn't seen a brush in years. The necklace looked like
billiard balls on a string and the pink pom-pom slippers
were so right that my feet ached as soon as I put them on.

The final bit of camouflage was applied with sponge
and brush under the guidance of a great expert, Bert Broe.
Bert has a shop down an alley off St Martin's Lane, just
up the road from the Coliseum and close to the hub of
London's theatreland. The shop is called the 'Theatre
Zoo'. In the window you'll find everything from a dragon's
head for a Chinese festival to the back end of a donkey for
a panto, as well as all the bits and pieces actors use as

make-up. Not just powder and greasepaint, but stick-on scars and warts.

I stood at the back of the shop for about ten minutes, waiting for Bert.

'Have you got any pregnancy stuffings?' enquired a girl.

'How far gone?' asked the assistant.

Nothing you could ask for here would raise an eyebrow. They had plastic axes for sticking through heads (some with bloody blades), vampire teeth and red rubber noses with added drips.

Bert appeared and we both sat in front of a mirror with light bulbs round the edge, and Bert looked long and hard at my face before jumping to any rapid conclusion. He reached for his pancakes and his powder like an artist for his tubes of oil.

'I'm going to get rid of your beard,' he said, and dabbed away. I was taking careful note since I would have to do all this for myself at the Lakeside.

'How high does your dress come?' asked Bert. 'In case I have to create a cleavage.'

I explained that with the boobs I had, I needed a cleavage like the Cheddar Gorge needs excavating!

Stage secret after secret poured out.

'Old pros used to get rid of their eyebrows with a bit of soap,' Bert told me. 'Put a bit of colour on your chin, it can easily get lost under the lights. Try some number nine. Try some bags under your eyes, use the brush, and draw some wrinkles on your forehead to suggest a few sleepless nights. You look great, you really do look great,' said Bert.

Actually, I did. I could not resist looking at myself in the mirror, pursing the lips and muttering, 'I'm not the woman I appear to be.' Surely this was going to bring the house down.

Marti Caine had told me to wear the lot, make-up and clothes, as often as possible. She said I'd get the 'mannerisms', so I did what I was told. A couple of mornings a week I would don the tent-like frock (not forgetting the boobs), drape the cardigan around me and stagger and shuffle around the house muttering, 'I'm not the woman I appear to be . . .' The cats would flee. Then the doorbell would go.

'*Don't answer it!*' my wife would scream.

On the inside, things were not much different. The message had hit home. If I firmly believed in this role, if I went out there saying to myself that I could make this audience laugh, then they *would* laugh. Believe in the part, believe in the jokes and success will follow. But confidence was too encompassing, for I still believed in myself too.

There's no problem parking a car at the Lakeside Club; all the spaces are Mercedes-width. The taxi-driver picked a spot as near to the stage door as he could get and unloaded a bag of clothes and an ironing board, and I staggered up the concrete steps – the longest, loneliest climb of my life.

I walked on to the stage for the first time at about three-thirty. It was for rehearsal. The producer of the stage show was called Max: round like a pudding, barking like a dog.

'I've got my ironing board with me,' I announced.

'This I've got to see,' said Max, astonished.

Before I had a chance to try even a couple of gags I was shunted off stage as fast as I'd been pushed on, and I went away haunted by the memory of those 800 empty velvet seats.

Then I bumped into Bernard Manning, unavoidable in these narrow backstage corridors. Bernard Manning is to clubland what Gaddafi is to world politics. Manning obeys no rules, will sink to any depth, twist any prejudice to get a laugh. He operates like a terrorist, and it is a brave man – or woman – who refuses to laugh in case the vengeance is turned on him.

'When you laugh, missus, your tits shake horrible,' he said to one woman who dared to sit, unsmiling, at his joke: 'Have you noticed how few Pakis there are since the Chinese discovered they taste like chicken?'

We stood face to face in the corridor, he in his underpants and enough spare gut hanging over the elastic to do for two others.

'Make 'em 'ave it,' he grunted like a disturbed pig, and he lumbered away to arm himself with a supply of deadly foul jokes to pump into his audience.

The Lakeside Club maintains its position at the head of clubland's league table by attracting a succession of stars. The Bernard Mannings, the Cannon and Balls, the Freddie Starrs and a host of other, even bigger, names that you probably won't have heard of unless you are a regular club-goer. Clubland has its own star system, paying no lip-service to television. You can be a big star in clubland, earn thousands a night and never have seen the inside of a television studio. The reverse is also true – being famous on TV is no guarantee of success here. As the man said, it's just like going into a bull-ring except that it's the audience who are the bulls: if you aren't fast enough on your feet, they'll gore you to death.

Exactly what might be to the taste of the Lakeside clientele is difficult to discover, though they certainly like things big, for it is an enormous aircraft hangar of a building upholstered with enough red velvet to reclothe the entire House of Lords. They also have a distinct taste for the artificial: everything from the created village atmosphere (plastic oak beams with stick-on knots in the unreal wood, and rural pantiles made into canopies over the Spanish-style bars) to the cream that oozes from the Black Forest Gâteau. The customers here are neither creators nor followers of trend: they are the producers of statistics. Prawn cocktail and well-done steak followed by gâteau is the best-selling menu in Britain today, and they're doing their best at the Lakeside to keep it on top. Broad gentlemen, sewn into their dinner jackets from an early age, man the doors to keep out 'unsuitables'.

It's lonely in your dressing-room before you go on. It may be crowded, as mine was, but that doesn't make any difference. Jimmy Perry was there, in a new suit; Beryl Reid had sent a telegram; Max was in and out, just checking – but none of them were any company. I knew I was on my own. As I started the make-up, I had to stop myself thinking how embarrassing, how shallow, how

unfunny it was going to be. I *had* to believe in me, and in
Ada, and in Jimmy's script. The doubts were still there,
but I wasn't afraid. I transformed all misgivings into
resignation and re-assured myself by saying, 'If this does
not go well, it will all be over in ten minutes, so what the
hell?' I was battening down my hatches, ready for any
storm.

I got the big build-up all right. The compère was not
backward in urging them to 'give a real warm welcome,
give a big hand for . . .'

There were bright lights from all directions, dazzling
enough to block out any view of the audience, but not of
the waitresses. It must have been the black and white
uniforms or the luminosity of the tomato soup they were
carrying that made them stand out. It didn't occur to me
at the time, but the tomato soup was another bad omen.
The funniest of funny men can't make you laugh when
you've got a mouthful of tomato soup. If only it had been
prawn cocktail: that doesn't require the same concentrated
effort as slopping soup.

The band gave me a fanfare, but within seconds of my
first pom-pom slipper shuffling on to the stage I knew it
was all over. They say you can sense death. I shuffled my
way to the ironing board – how pathetic that looked. Once
there, I had time to glance into the audience, hot cigar
ends shimmering like stars in the darkened auditorium. It
was not unlike being out at night alone, sensing but not
seeing others around you, wondering if they were hostile.

'I'm not the sort of woman I appear to be . . .' there
was a slight ripple, but difficult to be certain over the soup
spoons, '. . . to see me standing here, alluring and vital . . .'
audience unmoved, '. . . and her mother nagging him on
the other side, he's the only man down our street who gets
nagged in stereo.' Jimmy told me to wait for the laughs
before rushing on. So I waited. Nothing. 'And so many
double chins she looks as though she's peering at you over
the top of a pile of pancakes . . .' Nothing. But I wasn't
really expecting anything. Going out on stage is no different
from entering any room for the first time; you know if

you're welcome or not. I wasn't. They wanted to get on with their dinner.

On I trudged, like on the long march: '. . . from behind she looked like two small boys fighting under a blanket . . .' I tried a new technique with that one, looking a woman straight in the eye as I told it. She opened her mouth, only to stuff a buttered roll in it. '. . . She's so ignorant, she thought *Fiddler on the Roof* was Yehudi Menuhin putting up a television aerial . . .' There is a murmur running through the audience. It's not laughter. They're beginning to talk amongst themselves. '. . . I put my tongue out to lick my lips and somebody stuck a fork in it.' Bastards! Laugh! What was it Bernard Manning said? 'Make 'em 'ave it.'

The few who had been on my side early on, and had giggled a little at the first few jokes, had by now crossed to the other side and joined the silent majority. I made up my mind to have the only and the final laugh. I finished the routine, shuffled off the stage and came running back to take not one, but two curtain calls.

I said it was like an accident. Backstage the ghouls gathered to see the blood. Bernard Manning appeared from his dressing-room, his bulk casting a shadow.

'Look, son,' he said, 'I'd get out of the business if I was you. I've seen some deaths but that was the greatest. You should have got pinched for talking to yourself. You'd have got more laughs auctioning off the ironing board.'

Thank God for the moment just before I went on, the moment I finally realised that this was going to be a disaster. Without that, I would now have been totally crushed. I had given myself such a mental boost, gone so far in my belief in the character and the script, that without that premonition this aftermath would have been unbearable. But clubland is a hard school, and I had died a hard death – clubbed to death, if you like.

So who's to blame? Jimmy Perry for his misguided notion of what the clubland audience feeds on? Quaint little gags about piles of pancakes and the rest might have done well, as Ken Dod said, at a church hall or even a harvest supper, but not in clubland. When Bernard Manning is hitting them with stun-grenades, you can't hope to win with a pop-gun. But Jimmy's not to blame. These gags would have got laughs if Manning had done them, or Ken Dodd or Terry Scott. I've heard them since, similar ones anyway. They're old ones and the old ones are the best, if you can tell 'em. I can't quibble with any of the advice I'd been given on the way; it *is* all about believing, and selling yourself.

The blame must come to rest on me, not for any single mistake I made but for believing it was ever possible. I've never been the joke-teller at a party or in a pub, and here was my chance. Like the drunk who gets a laugh when his audience is half-sloshed, I was intoxicated by the smell of the greasepaint and the roar of the crowd. I believed they'd all laugh if they saw me in the drag, laugh at me like they do at a real comic.

It takes a nasty crash to cure a lousy driver, and it takes a nasty accident like the one I had at the Lakeside Club to curb an arrogant notion.

As Terry Scott warned me, 'You say, I'm sorry. I'll go and sweep the roads, but let me out of this agony.'

But my experience is not unusual. Every comic will tell you about the time he died. Some a dozen times or more. But still they go on, some suffer the humiliation for years, till a hint of stardom comes their way and makes it all worth while. Comics have been going through it ever since there have been stages for them to stand on.

And you still wonder why comics are sad men?

One Dog
and
his Man

One Dog and his Man

If this was to become one of the great friendships of all time, then we could have hoped for a more promising start.

For hours, the two of us motored through the night from his home in Bedfordshire to mine, in Suffolk. We exchanged the odd glance in the driving mirror but our eyes never met for long. I would occasionally ask him how he was, but got only a grunt in reply. It was early days yet; we had months in which to get to know each other, and if this first meeting passed without any upsetting incident then that was a good omen. Imagine how he must have felt, though – he had been plucked from his security and thrust into my inexpert care. Dog, they say, is man's best friend, but this treatment seemed to be stretching the relationship a bit far.

Tim was a fine-looking dog. Even the little bit of him that I could see in the driving mirror was impressive. His black, wet nose shone in the passing headlights, his distinctive border-collie white markings framed his dark face and eyes, and I fancied I could see in them the sorrowful look of an eternal refugee, for that is what he had been for the first seven years of his life. Born in Wales (or so we think), brought to Bedfordshire to be trained by the man who was also to train me, and then thrust into the back of a car and despatched to Suffolk in order that he and I might 'bond'. Talk about sheepdog trials! Poor old Tim. From the outset I felt as sorry for him as he clearly did for himself.

As guests go, although Tim did not know it, he had little to look forward to. I had been told quite forcibly that he should not be allowed to become a pet; no sight of the roaring fire for Tim but a chain and a kennel in the yard and only a bit of straw to make it home. Every meal would have to be fed by my hand to remind him who was master, every command must be obeyed, and within five months we *should* be able to read each other's minds. Telepathy, I was told, was the shepherd's secret and is the reason why, until they invent the intelligent tractor, there will be no better way of handling sheep than with a sheepdog.

It was late evening when we finally arrived home, Tim by now with crossed legs and his nervous new owner with crossed fingers, hoping the dog wasn't going to make a run for it as soon as the car door opened. He leapt out on the end of his stout leather lead and made the first of many territorial marks against the wheel of the car.

I fetched a length of old washing-line from the garage so that on his first night he would have sufficient, but limited, scope for roaming. I urged him into the kennel, a five-star billet compared to some; it had been a children's Wendy-house, but this did not impress Tim. He just sat and fixed me with large watery eyes that shone like motorway cats-eyes in the darkness. I left him there to fetch food and water, and as I walked up the path to the house I watched the two flashes of light follow my every move.

When I came back five minutes later, there was no dog. He had gone. The rotten old line had parted. I looked in the kennel. No sign. I shouted, 'Tim! . . . Tim! . . .' but he hardly knew my voice yet. Poor dog. I imagined him to be scampering off across fields in search of his old home two hundred miles away. Or worse: perhaps he'd found some sheep or cattle and started trying to boss them around in the darkness. A farmer might shoot him, I panicked, but remembered that where we live wheat and barley rather than beef and mutton are the crops, and even Tim seemed unlikely to mistake a combine-harvester for a flock of woolly sheep.

Then there was the money. Tim was a highly tuned and trained sheepdog. He had a pedigree which would have put him in the higher echelons of the Royal family if he had been born human instead of dog. There was a good thousand pounds' worth of border collie roaming around Suffolk, and all I could do was yell 'Tim . . . Tim' into the night.

'I've found him!' shouted my wife from the other side of the house. He had indeed returned home, but it was to the only home his tired and muddled mind recognised. The sad little dog was curled up, paw across his muzzle as if to hide from the world, almost asleep on the warm bonnet of the car that had brought him here. Our hearts went out to him and, with no resistance, he went back on his chain and was again shown the cosiness of his new kennel. But he didn't impress easily, and curled up on the cold damp earth as far away from it as his lead would allow. We went to bed a little fonder of Tim than we ever thought we might be at this stage.

The glow soon faded. It was about three o'clock in the morning when we woke to the sound of a low distant moan that would occasionally rise to a piercing crescendo. Ghosts? No, the cursed dog. We live some way off the beaten track so there are few neighbours, but this incessant howling and moaning would wake people in the village a mile away. We wrapped ourselves in dressing gowns and duffle coats and went out into the chill night to tell Tim that everything was all right.

Which it was, for about an hour, and then the ghostly chorus would start up again, moaning and sighing like a storm in the rigging of an old ship. In desperation we went to the fridge, took out a large lamb chop and flung it at him from the bathroom window.

So began one of the great love-hate relationships of my life – love and hate alternating often by the hour, sometimes by the minute.

I was torn: half of me longed to be a shepherd, the other half hated dogs. I had this vision of a peaceful man, tending his flock on the sun-dappled hillside and wandering alone across moor and fell in search of the one that had gone astray. He held no truck with modern farmers and their factory techniques, but rather earned his living from a deep understanding of nature given to him by the annual cycle of the birth and death of lambs. In the depths of the snowy, icy winter he would trudge with his lantern to where he thought he heard the pathetic bleat of a newly-born lamb: it would be rushed home, cradled in his arms, and placed next to the blazing fire until it was able to fend for itself.

I quite fancied all that, but dogs were a different matter. I hated them. At least, the ones I knew.

It's the owners that seem to be the problem. Dogs I have always suspected to be noble enough creatures; owners, most of the time, are not. Some pour bags of liquorice allsorts down the poor animal's gullet, others allow their dog to lick their face when it has just returned from the doggy-bowl full of stewed and pulverised offal. These are the people who get dogs a bad name with me. I dreaded becoming one.

But Norman Seamark was never going to be guilty of crimes such as these.

'A happy and contented dog is a dog that knows what it should be doing and how it should be behaving,' he told me early on in our relationship. And he practised what he preached. In his time as a top sheepdog trialist and, more recently, as president of the International Sheepdog Society, he has owned well over a score of border collies. Not one has ever set so much as a paw across his threshold. It is a brave dog that jumps up, as dogs do, in search of a quick stroke or cuddle, for they will be rebuked with an unaffectionate 'Get down.' And they *will* get down, because they know he means it. But they're happy dogs too. They know their place, and their job.

His task now was to exert a similar influence over me and school me as he schooled his dogs: to understand sheep, to understand the way they move and think, to develop a sense of anticipation. These are what it takes to win a sheepdog trial – these, and a good dog and a bit of luck.

Shepherds have a certain look about them, and Seamark was no exception. It's probably the weather that etches the furrow-like lines into their faces, and the sun that roasts their skin to the colour of hide. Then there's the stare: the piercing eyes that can see across fields and up hillsides and spot trouble a mile or more away. They're all fast walkers too, no gentle amble ever caught an escaping ram. Norman's fast bandy gait marked him out a mile off.

The look apart, nothing else about Norman Seamark could be fitted into the image of the shepherd. He has no hills and fells to patrol, but a richly cultivated 500 acres of Bedfordshire lowland where the chief landscape features are the airship hangars at Cardington and the distant forest of the London Brick Company chimneys. Sheep aren't his only source of income, either; half his farm grows highly profitable wheat and barley. He keeps sheep because they make him money, and if he is in any way fond of them he doesn't let on. After all, he loves his dogs dearly and still won't allow them in the house. At our first meeting, Tim rushed towards me and jumped up.

'He wants to play,' I said, half joking. 'No,' Norman rebuked me, 'it might have been play when he was a puppy, but it's now his work of a lifetime. The playing is over.' And he meant it.

Dogs have five basic commands, and using those alone you can place the dog exactly where you want him – and, consequently, the sheep. So goes the theory. One great advantage I had was that Tim was already schooled and knew what the words meant; obeying them was a different matter, but he knew what they meant.

To send the dog to his left you shout 'Come by', to his right 'Away here'. If you want him to stand still, you shout just that, 'Stand still'; if you think he should be moving closer to the sheep you tell him to 'Walk on', and if you want to call him off and bring him to heel, it's 'That will do', often abbreviated to 'That'll do'. What you have now is complete remote control. Wherever the dog might be, as long as he can hear you he should perform like a machine; the issuing of commands should be like pressing buttons. That was the theory, then we tried the practice.

Norman had brought about a dozen sheep into a piece

of land the size of a couple of football pitches, thankfully well fenced. It was close to the kennels, and as the sheep moved closer a barked chorus of anticipation rose from the other dogs. But this was not to be their day; it was Tim's. He sat at my feet, trying to lick my hand. I didn't discourage him but felt Norman's disapproving glare. Tim sensed it before I did and stopped.

'Send him off to gather up the sheep,' said Norman. I had to ask what the right word was, I'd forgotten already.

'You have to tell him to see his sheep. He might not have spotted them. As soon as he's seen them, tell him to 'come by' if you want him to go to the left, 'away here' if you want him to go to the right.'

I bent down close to Tim's floppy ear and told him: 'See your sheep.' He suddenly became taut, winding himself up. He saw them in an instant, and even at a distance of two hundred yards he twitched if one of them dared to move by so much as an inch.

'Come by,' I told him in a hushed voice and he was away like a sprinter off the starting blocks. He swung out in a large arc with the intention of creeping up behind the flock, but he'd not gone more than a few yards when they sensed him coming and slowly, as a flock, they started to move away, getting a little faster as he came closer.

They ran, faster. Tim chased them, faster and faster.

'What do I say to stop him?' I begged of Norman.

'Tell him to stand still. It's getting out of hand.'

'*Stand still!*' I barked like an angry sergeant major. And Tim rather reluctantly slithered to a halt. Except that it wasn't a complete standstill, more of a gentle creep forward. As he crept, so the sheep edged forward a little further. Within seconds, it was again up to the speed of a chase.

'Stand still!' I bellowed again, and once more he paused.

'Don't let him do anything that you don't want him to do,' warned Norman. 'If you do, he'll get out of hand and you'll never be able to control him. Having said that, don't be too firm. He's a bit timid by nature so don't be too severe with him. Just severe enough to let him know that you're in charge.'

While we were talking, Tim started his creep again.

I gave him the order to come to heel.

'*That'll do!*' I screamed, and indeed that would do for the first lesson.

'Are sheep stupid?' I asked of Norman, hoping they were.

'They do a lot of thinking,' said Norman. 'They'll weigh your dog up and look at him, and wonder if he's a strong dog and if he's really going to be boss. If they feel like it, they'll stamp their feet at him.'

I looked down at Tim. He was gone. At the far end of the field a small flock of sheep had broken into a gallop and a black and white hound was hotly in pursuit.

'*That'll do!*' I screamed for all I was worth. He gave one look in my direction, and ran on.

Tim was now living at home with me, and despite his early attempts at escape we had all settled down into unsettled routine. Unsettled for him, because all he wanted out of life was to chase sheep and we didn't have any, so he chased anything he could find. A plastic bag that was rolling along in the wind would seize his imagination, and he would slither on to his belly and fix it with a stare, and yap when it didn't respond. But these were highlights in what was otherwise a very dull life for him. We often felt as though we were being unkind, but on Norman's orders he was kept on his chain and firmly out of the house in case the temptations of the fireside rug should take his mind clean away from working sheep.

But he got plenty of walks. I had been given homework to do, and it was on the walks that we would practise. I would tell him to stand still and then I'd walk away as far as I dared, scolding him if he dared to move. Each day I would walk a little further. Then I would turn and look at him and scold him again if he flinched before I told him, 'That'll do.' Sometimes he would break my heart – sitting with his hangdog, forlorn look, longing to be back on his

farm and his native hillside. More often than not he would
infuriate us with his pointless yapping, and as the season
turned from winter into spring his morning chorus of
baying and whining moved from seven towards four
o'clock, woke the baby daily, and on bad mornings the
lamb chop thrown from the bathroom window was the
only remedy.

He had clearly formed a strong bond with the car after
that first journey home, and delight filled his eyes and set
his tail a-thrashing when I led him towards it. It meant
we were going back to Norman's, back to the sheep. For
my part, I was developing a reputation locally. Heads
turned as I walked through the Suffolk wheat-fields with
my sheepdog at heel, crook in hand.

'Here comes Bo-Peep,' they would say. 'He's lost his
sheep again.'

If you have never been to a sheepdog trial, as I hadn't,
it is bewildering: dogs and sheep running hither and thither
and long periods of inactivity broken only by a whistle or
a shouted command.

'It's not a circus act. Don't get that idea,' warned
Norman. He's right, of course. It's easy to believe that
what these men are asking of their dogs is an obedience
test, like the ones at Olympia where dogs do tricks in
tunnels and on see-saws. But trials aren't like that. What
the course represents is a typical day's work for a shepherd
and his dog. There's a bit of everything. The dogs have to
go and collect their sheep, bring them towards the shepherd
and drive them away between two stakes which might
represent a gate or a gap in a stone wall; they then have to
drive the sheep through what is called in the competition
'a Maltese cross' (which represents a sheep dip), and
finally shepherd and dog have to capture the flock in the
pen and close the gate on them. It's all against the clock,
as a day's work might be.

Dog and man will travel hundreds of miles to take part
in a trial. The first one we went to happened to be on the
Sussex downs, but there was an old man who had driven
all the way from Cumbria to take part. He set his dog off

at the start of the course, wasn't too pleased with the way the dog ran, called him back without finishing the course, got in the car and drove the 300 miles back to the Lake District. He hardly spoke a word to anybody, but shepherds must get used to a solitary life.

The crowds are of a reasonable size, the sort of numbers you might get for a well attended school sports day. Many casual spectators bring a dog with them, hoping that by watching it will learn some manners. And although the basset hounds and Jack Russells and the odd mongrel or two who sit on the boundary, restrained by a stout lead, have as much hope of rounding up sheep as you or I, nevertheless they watch every move and flinch at every shift of the sheep. The best attended stall is always the roast lamb on a spit – tactless, you'd think.

Even the experts get it wrong, though. Twice that day, top triallists set their dogs off from the starting post and didn't see them again till some hours later. You could just make them out, searching the woods at the far end of the field for the truant dog who had had more on his mind than sheep. Sometimes the sheep would just take fright. The one thing I had learnt about sheep so far was that if they are not in the mood to play, then you are in trouble. Instead of responding to the push of the dog like an amiable drunk might to a helping hand from a policeman, they will appear to panic and scatter. Which way they will go is anybody's guess. The only thing to do, it seemed to me at first, was to urge the dog on and let him catch them up. But I had tried this a few times and found it only made the sheep go faster, (a shepherd with his eye half on the balance sheet might worry about the amount of meat they were running off). The right thing to do is to stop the dog and let the sheep wind down on their own, but this calls for some courage because unless the dog is under perfect control (unlikely in my case) he will barge on. Either that or the sheep may disappear over the horizon. But in a sheepdog trial you're making this sort of decision every fifteen seconds or so. It makes for a busy ten minutes; the time limit in most trials.

I don't know how much you enjoy your job, but would you want to do it every weekend in the summer, as well as twelve hours a day during the week? Sheep dog triallists do.

'It's in your blood,' they will tell you, 'It's something you're born with. We love our sheep and our dogs. Give me a dog and some sheep and I don't want anything else in life.'

'Look at that white-headed sheep,' said Norman suddenly. He must be joking, they've all got white heads.

'No, that one there,' he said, pointing with his crook. We were watching the closing stage of a trial and the shepherd was doing his best to get the half dozen sheep into the pen, a box-like affair with a gate at one end, the whole thing being made out of hurdles and wooden fencing. The rules say that once you have picked up the string to open the gate, you cannot let it go till the sheep are in the pen and you have closed it behind you. That limits your scope severely since, as well as the dog, the threat of the shepherd's crook also has an influence on where the sheep go, and when you're effectively tied to the gate by the string there's only so far you can go.

You could see the man cursing as this one blessed, thick-skulled sheep resisted all attempts to be penned. The rest seemed quite happy to drift in, have the gate closed on them and call it a day, but she did not; and once she had sown the notion of disobedience, this poor chap did not stand a chance with any of them.

Round and round the pen they went, charging this way and that. No one would have blamed him if he'd picked up his stick and given them a good belt across the ear, but he didn't. He sweated it out, gradually exerting his will over them, till in the end man and dog brought the bad-tempered sheep into the pen. No panic, just a firm insist-ence and a lot of sheep sense. That's shepherds for you.

I had only two problems – controlling the dog and com-manding the sheep – and it was a toss-up as to which would be my downfall. It would depend very much on what happened on the day of my sheepdog trial, for the way the sheep behave and the way in which the dog performs are not entirely unrelated. Tim sensed when the sheep had got me beat. I knew from the instant Tim started to run towards them whether or not I was going to have an easy time; I suspect teachers have the same sort of sense – one look at the class and they know what they're in for. The sheep who fled were the biggest nightmare. I would send Tim off to gather a small flock, and he had only to take a couple of strides in their direction and a shudder would go through them; word travelled from sheep to sheep, and if they had worked themselves up to a gallop by the time Tim got there there was no chance either of him running fast enough or me being quick enough with my commands to bring order to the chaos. So I crossed my fingers and hoped that the sheep chosen for my trial required only an O-level in 'sheep sense'.

Tim had his problems too, although some of them I ought to blame on myself. The main one was that he didn't always do exactly as he was told – no great crime in a pet dog but in a sheepdog, a disaster.

It took an expert to analyse our mutual problem. We travelled to Wales, 300 miles for poor old Tim in the back of the car. On the long, tedious journey he would occasionally raise his head, look out of the car window in the hope of seeing a few sheep and, when he found there was only motorway whizzing by, he would return to his slumbers and dream.

We motored high into the Brecon Beacons to meet not only a breed of sheep that was new to us, but a kind of shepherd I had not met before: the upland sheep farmer.

Llystyn Farm, a white stone cottage clinging to a hillside some twenty miles north of Llandeilo, was a world apart from the groomed lowland sheep farms on which Tim and I had spent most of our time. There was no choice for the farmers here: the land was not good enough to grow anything other than grass for grazing, and even the small parcels of land that might be rich enough to grow lucrative corn would be too hilly, or be blemished by an outcrop of rock. The sheep led a different life too. In the summer months they might graze high on the hilltops, away from man and dog for weeks on end. It makes for a hardy sheep but also a timid one. 'Undogged', they call them; undoggable, you might say, for a man and his dog who have never faced such shy and unwilling beasts before.

The shepherds are hardier men too. They face harsher winters than their lowland counterparts, and work rougher ground, much of it without the benefit of wire fencing to keep flocks in one place at a time.

Gwilym Jones has farmed here all his life. Sheep are his work and sheepdog trialling is his pastime, in particular the brace competition. This is where two dogs are used instead of one. That might sound easier, but each dog has to be under individual command and, given that orders to one dog alone can fly around like machine-gun bullets, having to give orders to two seems almost impossible. But Gwilym is a champion, and his father before him.

He is short and speaks only occasionally with a broad Welsh accent, sometimes lapsing into Welsh. He wears a flat cap. There is a row of seven wooden pegs on the wall of the cottage; each carries a flat cap, one for each day of the week, a clean one for Sundays.

'I want you to go and gather those sheep from that field there.' He pointed with his crook to a field that looked empty. But because of the rise in the middle of it, the sheep grazing at the far end weren't visible from where I was standing.

'And I want you to bring them into this field here.' And he went away. No advice, no further comment – he just left me to it.

This was new to me. This wasn't pointless circling of a field, it was real work. It was like being a sprinter released from daily training on the track and told to run for a bus. I was a shepherd! I looked round for Gwilym, but he was back at the cottage. We were on our own.

I called Tim to heel.

'See your sheep,' I whispered, and he tensed.

'Come by,' I murmured, and away he ran to the left, striking out in an enormous arc to gather the sheep, most of whom were out of my sight on the other side of the hill.

Tim raced on till he was out of sight too. And then I waited. It might have been thirty seconds; it felt like thirty hours. First one black face appeared over the brow of the hill, then a dozen more. Not charging but walking steadily towards me. No sign of Tim, just sheep. How many? Perhaps three hundred – I was too wide awake to want to count sheep.

Then I saw half a dozen sheep sprinting madly in the opposite direction through a hedge and into an adjoining field. What now? Leave the flock of hundreds to their own devices while I sent Tim off to gather the strays? Would Tim obey anyway, at this distance? Tim was thinking faster than I was and was already in hot pursuit. The large flock came to a standstill, having sensed Tim's distraction, and the strays were now coming under his influence. He moved like lightning, displaying to the full his natural instinct, which was to bring a flock of sheep to the feet of his master. The few were gathered together and joined the many, and within a minute I was standing on a Welsh hillside in the middle of a flock of hundreds with Tim darting in every direction keeping them in place at my feet. I was proud of that dog.

Gwilym returned. He didn't say anything. It was a routine manoeuvre to him, but it was my first taste of real work, real shepherding.

We detached a few sheep from the flock; these were to be the ones with which I would put Tim through his paces. I went through the tedious routine: sent him to gather the sheep and then drive them away from me. I tried to get him to drive them in straight lines, but it lacked precision. It would have been perfectly good enough for a work-a-day performance, but not up to trial standard.

'You've got the same tone in your voice all the time,' said Gwilym, resting his crossed hands and his chin on top of his long crook. 'If you tell a dog to stand still and he doesn't obey, well, raise your voice. *Stand* . . . and if he doesn't do it, raise it a bit more. You've got to get more force into your voice. I can't stress that enough. You've got to be precise. Weigh every command and then the whole thing will come together.'

If I had any doubts as to whether it was me or Tim who was at fault, Gwilym set my mind at rest.

'There's nothing wrong with the dog. He's ideal. Smart dogs won't take orders, they're too tender. But he's fine. He's the sort of dog that can win a trial.'

Listening to Gwilym, I had failed to keep an eye on Tim. Gwilym hadn't.

'Look, he's roaming around. I wouldn't let my dog do that.'

I called him towards me and he came.

'That's right. Keep him at your heel. Look . . . he's starting to wander already. Keep him there.'

I shouted at him again.

'Don't let him off the hook. Don't let him take a step you don't want him to take.'

I shouted again. He wandered off.

'*Stand there!*' barked Gwilym with a roar that echoed down the valley. Tim froze, and would still be there if I hadn't called him to the car.

'A word of advice,' offered Gwilym as we were about to leave. 'Don't worry about your dog. Get him under control and forget about him, and when it comes to your trial watch the sheep and only the sheep.'

I had 400 long and tedious motorway miles in which to practise my intonations before Tim and I would be on show again. To all the drivers between home and Scotland who thought I might have been swearing at them, I humbly apologise. No offence was meant if I yelled 'Come by' at you as you overtook. Poor Tim, in the back, must have been very confused, and for most of the journey took the option of sleeping.

We were off to see the Billinghams, Geoff and Viv. Again, they were shepherds of a kind I had not met before. They were a husband and wife team, which was unusual in itself, but unlike the others they weren't landowners with flocks of their own but servants of the Duke of Roxburghe and part of a team of a dozen or so shepherds who tended the Duke's sheep on his countless wild acres on the Scottish borders.

The Billinghams live in a remote spot. Many miles down a lane which goes nowhere, along the bottom of a valley between steep hillsides which will grow only bracken, heather and the occasional patch of grass, you come to a small stone house. Scores of dead moles are strung out along the wire fence; evidence to the Duke in the unlikely event of his passing this way that the molecatcher was doing his job.

Geoff is fair, tall and fit. Gently spoken, he has a picturesque habit of bending down on one knee to watch his dog and then supporting his weight with his hands on his crook, a Biblical pose. Viv is an unlikely girl to be a shepherd – blonde, bubbly and determined to make her mark in a man's world.

Around the kitchen stove, we settled down to a farm-house tea. Scones, jam, thickly sliced bread, strong tea and long tales of winter. This is a part of the country where bad weather dominates and summer is a mere respite from the frost and snows of the long, harsh winters.

'It's in the winter you feel closest to your dogs,' said Geoff. 'If it weren't for your dogs you'd be on your own. You're out there in a snowstorm and you know you've got to find your sheep. You can't see him but your dog can smell them and he'll take you to them.' A look of pride comes over his face. 'Last winter there was a sheep in a ditch and it was completely covered with snow and sinking further and further. But the dog found it and actually got hold of it by the neck wool and was starting to drag it out.'

'You can breed a strain of dog that's almost human,' added Viv, 'and that dog will actually know what you're thinking. At lambing time, for example, if he sees a ewe in trouble, perhaps the lamb's too big for her or something, he'll automatically stop and look at the ewe, then he'll glance at you as if to say, "Look! There's a ewe in trouble. Do you want me to catch it?"'

The praise and love of the border collie pours out of them. They might have been talking about their own children.

'You couldn't be a shepherd without a dog,' said Geoff. 'You get whizzkids these days who drive around on fast motorbikes and gather up the sheep that way. But they'll never replace the dog. Dogs can use their brains, machines never can.'

Geoff and Viv have some of the finest dogs in the country, and a shelf crammed with medals and cups to prove their skills at trialling. If they wanted, they could join the growing band who have exploited the newly found public love for the border collie and breed dogs that would command thousands of pounds when fully trained. The Billinghams could be comfortably off if they wanted to be.

'I won't make money from dogs,' said Geoff. 'I couldn't send a friend down the road for a thousand pounds. How can you put money in your pocket and see a friend walk away?'

We scrambled down the hill from the house to some small fields hedged in by stone walls. This was where the ewes were gathered who were having late lambs. Halfway there, Viv stopped and watched one particular ewe who was walking shakily in small circles in a corner of the field.

'If you want to be a shepherd, you might as well deliver your first lamb,' she said, and before I had chance to say no – my immediate reaction – we were kneeling by this ewe who was now lying down and grunting.

Through a thick layer of semi-transparent blood-spotted membrane I could just pick out two black feet, the first part of the lamb to be born.

'Get hold of it,' urged Viv, not giving too much thought to what I was doing. The feet were warm, very warm. The unborn part of the lamb I could feel, still struggling away inside.

'Give the old girl a bit of a hand . . . pull . . . gently . . .' More lamb emerged, the grey woolly coat matted and blood-stained. Then, in a rush, the whole animal was born. It looked dead. Hardly a movement except for an occasional twitch, and no eye movement. I didn't look closely enough to see if there was any breathing.

'Pick it up by the back legs,' said Viv. I did. Poor little thing, hanging there as it surely would from a butcher's hook in six months' time. Viv took it from me and slung it to the mother's head, the mother still post-natal and prostrate.

'She's got to get the smell of it or she'll reject it when it starts to feed.'

Slowly, with a forceful lick from its mother, the lamb came to life.

'Sometimes the ewes just clear off and leave the lambs,' said Viv. 'What we do then is to tie her legs together so she can't get up. That way she has to get used to the lamb.' Not much evidence of high-tech childbirth in the lambing pens.

The lamb safely delivered, we strolled back to the house. I felt pleased with myself. I called Tim and he came bounding along behind. I turned to talk to Viv, and just as we were about to walk off Viv shouted. 'Call your dog off,' she was nearly screaming, and ran across to where Tim had something in his mouth which he was violently shaking from side to side, worrying. I didn't know what it was, but Viv realised in an instant.

When she got there, the lamb was dead; not the lamb we had just seen born, but a sickly little thing born earlier that day and confined to this small field in the hope that it might survive. We speculated as to what might have happened. Tim wasn't an aggressive dog, and it seemed to be odd behaviour for a dog of his character. Perhaps he thought it was dead already; it's not unusual for sheepdogs to eat up afterbirth left lying around the fields.

'I don't want you to worry about it,' said Viv, 'you've helped your first lamb into the world today. You've given us one, and taken one away. That's all.'

We arrived back in Bedfordshire, at Norman Seamark's farm, for the last training session before my trial, which was to be held in the grounds of Woburn Abbey. This was to be the final briefing to the troops before we went over the top.

'Your voice has come along nicely,' said Norman. 'You're getting the various inflexions and you can now use them to put more pressure on him when you want to. You also know when to ease off him, and that's good.'

Other bits weren't quite so good.

'He's tending to bore on you, push at you a bit, so you've got to be firmer when you're working close to him. There's no room for error. When you get those sheep going in circles round the pen instead of going into it, you're in dead trouble.'

Sheep sense?

'Yeah, that's coming along. Since I told you to watch your sheeps' heads and see which way they move, you've got better control of them. When the heads move, stop your dog because he's done his job. He's turned them. Let them go on and keep watching the heads, because it's the heads that move before the body does. Let's hope you get good sheep on the day because, be under no illusions, the best man and best dog might as well retire and go home if it's four bad sheep that come out of the pen.'

I knew he was right, of course. Some of Norman's sheep, the ones I'd been training with, were almost tame. They were so used to the sight of the dogs and to the training routine that they often obliged by going through the motions. But when he swapped those for a flock who hadn't seen dogs so recently, I could easily get into trouble. I've stood for twenty minutes holding open the gate of the pen while the four sheep have refused to go in and have paraded in circles instead, seeing which of us would get dizzy first and retire. Usually it was me.

Trial day was bright but not too breezy, which was good since shouted commands can easily get lost in a strong wind. Tim and I piled out of the car and went over to have a look at the course. There was a thin line of spectators – a few hundred, typical for a sheepdog trial. One or two familiar faces were there, some of the old boys who had travelled hundreds of miles to have one run at the sheep. Dogs were tied by strong leads to bumpers of cars which were flexing as anxious dogs strained to get at the sheep. There were well over fifty competitors, which makes for a lot of sheep since each competitor gets a new flock of four: you don't get the same sheep going round and round like a stage army, as I used to think.

We had time to kill before we were due to go to the post, a stake hammered into the ground from which the competitor should not move more than a few feet. The ground sloped upwards from the stake, so the sheep would be running downhill towards me. The flock had to be gathered up from the far end, brought down the course and through a gateway, just to ensure that your dog can bring the sheep towards you in a straight line. You then had to swing them behind you and command the dog to drive them away towards another gate to test your aim once again.

Then the cross-drive. This is said to be the real test since all the dog's instincts are to bring the sheep back towards you, not across you. So the sheep are driven across the field, through another gate, and then back to the centre of the field and to the Maltese Cross, a man-made obstacle in the shape of a cross with an alleyway through the centre.

But before the cross, there were trees to negotiate. I hadn't come across this before. There was a slalom to execute between giant oaks, and it was uphill as well! If we got through that, then we had to get the sheep through the Maltese Cross and then on to the pen. Once they were inside the pen, the trial was over. I prayed for it to be soon.

My name was eventually called from the loudspeaker, and I let Tim off his lead and walked with him to the post. The judge waved the white flag which was the signal for the four sheep to be released at the other end of the field. They were a long way away. I could hardly see them, but

Tim sensed them and stood rigid. I whispered, 'Away', and gave him a 'Sssshh' to urge him along. There was nothing I could do now. Tim ran out to the right, but until he had made contact with the sheep it was all up to him. He ran and ran; it must have been a quarter of a mile. What I had feared came to pass. On seeing Tim the sheep bolted, charging off as if a gun had been fired. If Tim didn't catch them the trial would be over. It was going to be difficult enough with sheep as touchy as this, but touchy sheep were better than no sheep at all. Tim ran faster. The trial was moving into a higher gear than this sport was designed for, certainly faster than I could deal with. The post is a lonely place when both the sheep and your dog are out of sight and you are scanning the field for the first sight of movement which tells you the dog has caught them. It was a miracle he'd recognised them as being sheep. Freshly shorn, they looked more like goats. And that was the root of our problem – the sheep were feeling cold and having Tim upon them was only making them crosser.

Tim eventually caught up and took charge and brought the sheep down the field, but the lines weren't very straight and we missed the gate: lots of marks lost, but we were still in the game.

However, the sheep didn't stop. They ran on, faster and faster, and if I had been a second later in giving Tim a command he would have failed to head them off and they'd have been through the crowd and away. Poor Norman. What must he be thinking? On they charged, still at full belt but in more or less the right direction, with Tim in hot pursuit.

Stupidly, I gave him one command too many and just missed another gate, but despite all obstacles put in our way we were still in the competition. That's more than a lot of competitors could have said; the list of retirements had grown longer as the day wore on.

Then the cursed beasts decided to go their own way. One lousy sheep ran to the left, the other three dived off to the right. It was slap in the middle of the trees too: the trickiest bit of the course. To hell with the single, I decided, and sent Tim off in pursuit of the other three. I felt a tap on the shoulder. The judge had left his tent to pluck me from the mire into which I was sliding.

'Go and get the stray, get them all together again, calm down and then carry on.'

I detached Tim from the trio and sent him to find the loner. The loner spotted Tim and, seeing his friends not far away, decided the easiest thing was to rejoin them. Thank God. Now on to the Maltese Cross.

Most would have given up by now. The sheep were at boiling point, panting, frightened perhaps, but unfortunately they weren't knackered, which might have slowed them down a bit. With few marks gained for the manoeuvres in the trees, I decided to live for the moment and make as good a job as I could of the rest. If I got them in the pen at the end, I would go home happy.

They charged down the hill and right past the alleyway in the Maltese Cross through which Tim and I were supposed to drive them. I headed them off by brandishing my shepherd's crook (which you are allowed to do providing you don't hit them with it) and they came to a halt. For the first time in many minutes, Tim obeyed an order and he came to a halt as well. For a good fifteen seconds we all took deep breaths.

Then, slowly, surely and gently, I placed Tim to ease the sheep up to the Cross. First one way and then the other, heading them off whichever way they might try and go. Miracle of miracles, they came to a halt at the entrance. I was like a golfer who sees the ball come so close to the hole that the next shot can't fail. I ordered Tim to freeze. If we frightened them now, we'd never get them through. I banged the stick on the ground once or twice, just to let them know I was there and, with almost a whisper, I told Tim to 'walk on' and just give the sheep enough momentum to persuade the first one through – one through and the rest would follow. All four were in the alleyway now, and the first one stopped. I banged the stick and nothing moved. I moved Tim closer to pressurise them, and they reluctantly went on till they were through the Cross.

Then, sick not only of me but of the dog, they turned to face Tim in defiance. They dared him to come any closer. He took up the challenge, rushed forward, gave the trouble-maker the slightest of nips on the nose and, having re-established his authority, gave chase again.

I ran across the field after Tim and the sheep, trying to shout commands as I went and hoping to stop them before they ran past the pen – the final obstacle.

I was in charge by now, and Tim sensed some kind of victory; if not a points win it was going to be a moral triumph, and with little effort we again brought the sheep to a halt at the mouth of the pen. I let them stand. Having got this far I wasn't going to blow it. We put the pressure on, Tim and I working together as we never had before. Step by step the sheep edged through the gateway and, with a final tap of the crook on the ground behind them, they were in. I slammed the gate shut, gave Tim the hug of his life (although he wasn't in the slightest bit interested) and walked off the course to loud applause, most of it intended for Tim.

Norman was the first person I met. He had suffered as much as I had. He'd been a competitor earlier on in the day and had been forced to retire, so he knew what I'd had on my hands. There was a lot of praise from countless shepherds who told me they hadn't done as well on their first trial. There was a lot of post-mortem too: how I should have cooled the action down earlier on, how I should have taken control sooner, how Tim knew more about the job than I did and so on. None of this mattered.

I had entered the trial not caring whether I got good points or bad; I just wanted to pen the sheep, score the final goal, bring them home like a working shepherd might. In three months I had learnt to do it.

But what about Tim? How could I bear to part with him, my travelling companion for over two thousand miles, the dog with whom I had worked until his mind had become an extension of mine?

To those who say I was heartless to part with him, to those who shed a tear of their own when they saw Norman Seamark take him away, let me describe to you Tim's face every time I led him to the car to take him home to his boring Suffolk kennel after a day out with Norman's sheep or on a Scottish or Cumbrian fell. The sadness in his eyes was unbearable. Tim was bred to work. He knew no other joys than being on the farm, in the open, gathering a flock. The cruellest thing would have been to take him away from all that, to an alien life of patting and brushing and cossetting. His home was on the farm and that's where he is now . . . and good luck to him. He earned it.

Hair Today,
Gone Tomorrow

Hair Today, Gone Tomorrow

September

One day, between now and Christmas, I shall pick up a pair of scissors. Any other week and it might have been to slice the rind off a piece of bacon, or release from captivity a blister-packed chop. But this week, when steel meets steel in a pincer movement co-ordinated by my uncertain fingers, I shall be changing the direction of a life. Whose life, I cannot be certain at this stage. It will be either mine or, more likely, that of the poor woman who will sit before me.

To reassure the squeamish, this is in no way a medical assignment (although I cannot guarantee that there will be no blood – tears perhaps, sweat undoubtedly, but blood I shall do my best to avoid). No, this is merely the cutting of a lady's head of hair. And what might make that commonplace operation in any way out of the ordinary? The answer divides itself into two – me and her.

Me first: I have never cut a head of hair in my life. That needn't worry me (or her) unduly, because I have been promised the very best of tuition. But my problem goes far deeper than mere lack of ability, it goes to my very soul; I don't understand women's obsession with their hair and, to be frank, I'm not really interested. If the solution to this dilemma requires an understanding of style, of fashion, of what 'looks good' I'm in bigger trouble than I thought, for I have an eye for fashion like a drunk has an eye for mineral water. I have never tried it, have no use for it, can't begin to see the thrill in it. Deep down, I'm a short-back-and-sides man who believes that the highly stylish 'crumpled' look is due to a sudden shortage of steam irons, and the fashion for gashes and tears in quite respectable pieces of cloth is due to a sudden revolt by spin driers. As for hair, I rather tend to assume that the pink, green and blue spikes of rigid, threatening hair that appear on apparently sane people's heads are being worn for a bet.

Now 'her', poor woman. I can't suspect why she is letting me do this to her. The strange thing is that although we have never met, I know what her hair is like; it has been decorating various newspapers for fifteen years or more and, because the postage-stamp-sized byline pictures are always head and shoulders, the undistracted mind ends up knowing little about this woman other than the style of the hair. Rather like a light under a bushel, she hides under a mop of tumbling blonde (going on pale mouse) hair falling over one eye in piratical style. Apt, for much of her writing has a touch of the renegade about it – more a Captain Pugwash, though, than a wicked Cap'n Hook. When she turned away from hard-edged journalism to slide between the silken covers of romantic fiction, the hard torrent of blonde gave way to a more gentle waterfall effect, with a fringe that cascaded to just above the eye. What it's like round the back, God only knows. The little pics never show that.

To sum up: a poor brave woman is going to let me loose on her trademark. I take my hat off to her. I only hope she will feel able to do the same.

She is Jilly Cooper.

I'm past the stage where going to school means name tags sewn into caps, dinner money pressed into palm, gym shoes forgotten and rushed home for. I'm past having to endure all that, but the sensation of a first day in a new classroom does not change over thirty years. This is day one at the Vidal Sassoon school of hairdressing.

The school hides itself down a mews a hair's-breadth away from Bond Street. All is grey – Sassoon grey. Grey walls with Sassoon writ large in darker grey letters, grey gowns to catch falling grey hair, with sometimes a splash of daring black to lighten the effect. Even some of the towels are grey, rejects from the smart West End salons now reduced to wraps on to which the first locks I shall ever cut will fall. 'Battleship grey' springs to mind, and I mentally batten down my hatches and prepare for conflict.

I am introduced to Richard, who is to be my personal tutor. His black leather lace-up boots with thick spongey soles are just like those my old Dad wore when he drove a lorry for the Coal Board. Richard's trousers don't fit; sloppy, my dad would have called them. They are about five feet wide at the waist and gathered together by a large leather belt with the resulting surplus allowed to hang over the top, giving them the look of a frilly curtain. I think the tailor lost his scissors halfway through this pair. There seems to be enough cloth left over to make turn-ups big enough to carry the clue to a hundred Sherlock Holmes mysteries. Funny to have such deep turn-ups and stop the trouser leg four inches short of what my old Dad and I would have considered smart.

Being smart is my first big mistake. Smartness means nothing, style means all. So my smart black trousers, well pressed shirt and tidy beige casual jacket stand out here like cycle clips at a Hunt Ball.

I start to look around, but soon realise this is not necessary since all four walls are clad entirely in mirrors. Nor is looking around very comforting, for comparisons only upset me. What slender waifs these all are, lean enough to get two of their legs down one of my trouser legs. It is a small room, no bigger than a kitchen. Seven students are cutting seven models, and Richard is watching every single hair fall. Having taken in his clothes, and trying to understand why one young man is wearing his mother's old overcoat over his jeans, which are cut in such a way as to bring the crutch down to knee level, I get a chance to clock Richard's face. He looks a kind chap. Let's hope.

There's a tool-kit that goes with the job, and goes very quickly if you don't keep your eyes on it. It's like a doctor's bag and stethoscope; they should, I am told, become very personal to you, the tools of your trade. There's not much to these kits (kept incidentally in tool-rolls, rather like engineers keep oily spanners); it's not what you would call a versatile set of equipment – a Swiss Army penknife has more functions. There are two combs, in grey of course: one ordinary-sized one and another with teeth big enough to rake through a lion's mane. Two brushes with nylon teeth fairly close together, and a couple with spiky teeth a long way apart. And that's it – the entire haircutter's armoury except for the mystical scissors themselves, and these are closer to a crimper's heart than his old Granny.

'I know when someone's been using my scissors,' said one student with a gravity reminiscent of Daddy Bear sniffing over his plundered porridge bowl.

'Drop 'em and they're useless. They have to be reset,' warned another. I find all this a little difficult to believe.

And of course there's the hand-held blowdryer. It is with this in hand that I begin the long march that will eventually lead to Jilly Cooper's hair. Dryer in the right hand, brush in the left, a couple of hairclips slipped up my sleeve (and a little sweat on my brow), I get my first lesson in blowdrying. It is fundamental to hairdressing, although I must say it seemed a little strange to be starting at the end of the whole process.

'It will get you used to handling hair,' urged Richard, and with a magician-like flick of his comb and wrist he gathered in his hand what is known as a 'section' of wet and untutored hair and laid it across the teeth of the brush. 'Keep your dryer *up* . . . brush smoothly down through the hair . . . and . . . twist . . . and out. Flick the brush over, run it back to the top of the section . . . *twist* and . . . down again. Keep your dryer *up*!'

I promised earlier on not to be medical about this whole business, but I do find something about it which smacks of dentists; it's the gowns and the heads, held back, and the small but determined selection of weapons that sit on the table by the side of your client. That's a word I'm learning to use: client. 'The lady' is used a lot as well. There is clearly a need to talk above the head of one's patient, sorry client, and so 'the lady' is always referred to – as in 'the lady would like her fringe a little shorter . . .' or 'the lady thinks the blowdryer is too hot and is coming out in red blotches'.

And so the blowdrying proceeds, with brushful after brushful taken until the soggy clump of hair is once again straight and as smooth as a well groomed horse, as flat as if moulded to the head. Static can be a problem; get the hair too dry and bits fly here, there and everywhere. They're going to anyway, as soon as the haircut hits the streets of London, but I am beginning to understand that haircuts are done for the benefit of the salon mirror, and if it falls happily on 'the lady' that's a bonus. This seems to be true in the school anyway, where all manner of girls are persuaded into trims and trimmings that might never have crossed their minds. It has to be said that most go away happy. Surprised sometimes, but happy. But never with static, not my ladies anyway. Some other teacher, not Richard, told me to turn away from 'the lady', spit into your hands, rub them together and then run the damp palms over the head of hair. I am often tempted to try it, but decide to wait till a 'madam' rather than a 'lady' sits before me and then I shall sneak into a corner and . . .

I'm far from happy. Blowdrying is relentlessly boring. Brushful after brushful, on a thick, long head of hair – it is as tedious as breaking out of jail with a nailfile.

Five days on, however, and we make a breakthrough – we move on to cutting. And not on wigs either, much to my surprise. These are real ladies lined up to let me lop off their locks. Straight hair only, mind; no curls for a good few weeks yet. Shampooing is the first stage. They tell you there's art in this and that is why youngsters who start off as 'juniors' spend about three long years doing it (as well as making stylists tea and developing a close relationship with the broom). But I can't see what all the fuss is about. A couple of squirts from the shampoo dispenser and then the 'lady' gets the same sort of treatment from me as my mother's dog might. The ladies don't seem to complain, and I am often tempted to push my luck just to see how many gallons of rinsing water I can pour down an earhole before it protests.

'Watch the make-up. Don't let it dribble down the face. It'll leave little rivers,' orders a teacher, 'some of our ladies wear quite a bit of make-up.' You're not kidding. To those whose Elizabeth Arden masks became Nile-like deltas, I apologise (in nearly every case).

But the women worry me a lot. After thirty or more blowdrys and a few initial stabs at cutting, I am forced to the conclusion that the scissors and comb are the least of this job. It is not penetrating the hair, but the thick skull beneath it, which is the major hurdle to overcome before you can call yourself a hairdresser.

Take, for example, the ones who announce that 'You can do what you like, I don't care.' They are invariably the ones who care most, and not just for the end product; every single hair has to be cut and preened to the entire satisfaction of their supposed indifference. And as for the *carte blanche* to do as you wish, just try! The smelly ones take some handling too, for successful cutting calls for the elbow to be bent – not easy when trying to operate at arm's length. Sometimes it's fish and chips that wafts upwards as the heat of the blowdryer brings out the collected odours of their day's labours, sometimes a lingering memory of fried onions.

There was a time when this perpetual parade of scents might have set my gastric juices a-swirling, but I am beginning to overcome the need for food and drink. This is not entirely voluntary, but none of the other students seem ever to put lips to coffee cup between half-past eight in the morning and noon, and many will ignore the lunch break in favour of an interesting head. I would feel a little conspicuous with a flask of tea and a ham salad roll while all around me showed devotion to the female scalp, and so I wean myself from being a four-cup-a-morning man to zero. The first few weeks of my training are hence marred by a nervous tic which has developed in my left arm, which seems to be suffering from caffeine-withdrawal symptoms.

Then come the Japanese girls. These are vital to my

training, since oriental hair is fine and straight and it is straight haircuts on which I am starting. They make perfect 'bobs'. Bobs are where the hair falls from the parting to finish on a precisely cut line as smooth and as accurate as if it was done with a bacon-slicer. Early attempts produce more of a tin-opener effect, but I am learning, and Japanese girls seem perfect to practise on. Not only is their hair straight, but few seem to have any grasp of English and cannot understand my muttered oaths.

Old ladies can be a problem. They *really* don't care what you do. Most seem to want to spend as long as they can in the warm. Perhaps the blowdryer has replaced the coalfire in their lives – something warm and comforting to gather round and have a cosy chat. I've met rich girls, poor girls, models and ladies of all classes, and the only one who ever offered me a tip was the old lady who could least afford it. She was the one who kept falling asleep, and as her head nodded forward, so my lines became more ragged till I was forced to use the cold water handspray to wake her up.

But the worst are the dieters. These are the girls who present themselves at the school in the middle of the morning and who clearly have not eaten for at least forty-eight hours before. If they have, it is only to suck on a lemon or sip at a cup of tea made with one pass of a teabag. A couple of hours into the haircut (which is roughly a third of the way through at my present rate), there will be a sudden request for a breath of fresh air. This will be duly taken and a little tinge of pink will return to ashen cheeks, but you know that it is only a matter of minutes before the next request. And so it can go on: a self-perpetuating process, for such interruptions slow down the haircut and the longer the lady sits, head forward, in the stuffy atmosphere of the classroom the more frequent become the breaks 'for air', till the end-result of all this will be the first ever blowdry to be done with the lady on a ventilator.

Five weeks on and I'm getting good. At least, they think

I'm getting good and, though it pains me to admit it, I am beginning to dislike this whole business less and less. I have learnt to approach each head in the same way that a clock repairer might, or a jeweller, and throw myself into a salvaging job. My lines are getting straighter and I am just beginning to develop that first characteristic of a professional hairdresser – the ability to blowdry, talk drivel and look elsewhere at the same time. Even the feet aren't playing up any more. The perpetual dull ache in the lower leg that haunted me for the first couple of weeks has gone, and I greet each new client with a genuine smile (American girls chewing gum excepted; too much jaw movement causes poorly cut lines, which in turn results in a further torrent of jaw movement). I have yet to clout anyone round the head with the blowdryer, but it is my *soirée* shortly and I fear the pressure will bring out the worst in me.

The *soirée* is an evening of fierce competition disguised as an entertainment. Students of all grades and abilities parade the haircuts they have done that day, often under pressure of time and space, in front of an invited audience of cheering students, critical tutors, haughty and distant fashion editors and a few proud parents. The *soirée* is designed to be eye-catching, and the particular eye that the students have in mind is that of a prospective employer. Many are called to the Vidal Sassoon school, but few are ever chosen to go on to work in Sassoon salons. The lucky ones will, or might, end up in other West End shops, but for the rest it's High Street Here I Come. Hence, *soirée* night has an added piquancy.

I'm ready for it. I'm down to three hours per haircut now (professionals get about half an hour). All looks well. My model has good straight black hair, a sheen to it, a face that will match the starkness of my cut (although I do not pass this compliment on first meeting) and all is set fair. Until she opens her lipsticked mouth.

'I don't want much off. How much will you take off?' and so the whine goes on. 'Only a couple of inches . . .

only a couple . . .' I croon like a needle stuck in a groove. 'I've got my career to think of,' she protests.

'And I've got a haircut to do,' I retort, and desperately try to explain that the beauty of the bob is the geometrical shape, the straight line, the unbroken fall. You wouldn't ask Euclid to work with a wavy ruler, why should I bow to this pressure to cut longer than will look perfect to the judge's eyes? Whose hair is it, hers or mine?

Richard appears, sensing tension. 'Look, you agreed to have it cut, now sit down and *have* it cut!' The old Sassoon charm drains down the plughole like the shampoo suds.

A girl student from Barnsley, also hell-bent on a good showing in the *soirée*, is working next to me. She pulls me to one side to give me the benefit of her experience: 'Just sit her down and cut the bugger off!'

I do just that. And pretty well too, despite a constant stream of questioning which I follow up with a constant stream of hollow reassurance. I honestly haven't got a clue how it is going to end up, but I know the manoeuvres I have to go through to produce the shape that I want. I'm afraid my approach is rather that of the stage German Army officer – I do it all by the rule book.

When it is done, I dutifully flit round the back with the mirror so she can see that I have modelled my lines on the old Roman roads. She nods. 'I like it. Do you know, I think this is better than the length I wanted it at!' Richard intervenes just as the hairdryer is about to descend on her contrary skull.

My judges are waiting: Christopher and Philip. Christopher Brooker is the International Creative Director and Philip Rogers is the money and management man – International Creative Accountant perhaps. Brooker is one of Sassoon's boys made good, having learnt his craft in the sixties when Sassoon invented the 'wash 'n wear' style of haircutting as opposed to the 'wash, spray, brush, comb and don't-move-your-head' style that had been made famous by Mr Teazy Weazy and had reigned supreme until then. Slight and shy, Brooker now jets around the world with almost as much speed as he dances round a salon chair, hands and fingers flying.

He also panics, but understandably. When we first met, he asked me to demonstrate my prowess with brush and comb. A few seconds of watching and he dived to the phone. 'I want him to have three, no four, no *five* models every day he's in the school and I want to be told how he's getting on wherever I am in the world,' he barked.

The judging is like an identity parade, with Brooker walking along the line avoiding all contact with the face and looking forensically at the hair, searching for a clue which might make one the winner. Rogers sits, directing his sharp features everywhere but at no one in particular, and says little. But he sweats a lot, realising the cost to his company if this school of worldwide reputation shows itself unable to teach fat fingers like mine to sculpt hair.

'You cut a mean line,' says Brooker, looking relieved. Is he using that word to indicate 'average' or 'miserly'? No, he means 'good' and gives me third place out of eight. It is recognised by all concerned as a triumph. 'He's third because he came third,' asserts Brooker to indicate that he was in no way swayed by my privileged position. Rogers mops the sweat from his brow and breathes again.

In the most false display I have ever made in my life, I kiss my model and thank her very much. In one of the most honest displays of gratitude, I thank Richard, who has taught me so much in so little time and brought me so far. It has been eight weeks now. Loathing has not yet turned to loving, but I am acquiring an appetite for cutting hair. The throb of the varicose vein after an eight-hour day no longer worries me. Each head of hair is a new challenge, and I greet each lady not with a look into her eyes but with a scan of her hair. Watch out, boy! You are getting deeper into all this than you ever thought possible.

It may have been a long, hard climb so far, but I am still only on the foothills. I have still to ascend the mighty peak that crowns the head of Ms Jilly Cooper. What is so special about her? Why should her locks present more of a challenge than those of the somnolent old lady? The answer is that she is a 'celeb', and in our star system we like to think that *they* are not like *us* and so, in some mysterious way, her hair presents more of a challenge than yours or mine. That is one argument. The other, and more pressing reason, is that she will be presenting the supreme trophy at the British Hairdressing Awards at the London Hilton in six weeks' time and Brooker requires her hair to look 'shit hot'. There will be a ballroom full of fiercely competitive top London stylists, any one of whom could teach a dozen Hollywood stars the meaning of professional jealousy.

There are three major hurdles before I can transform what has been described as her 'Goldilocks look' into what Sassoon's call 'a wild look, a head of hair like a lion's mane'. The first hurdle is the lady herself, who must be persuaded. The second is her husband who, I am told from the horse's mouth, 'only married me for my long hair', And finally, and most at the forefront of my mind, is the hurdle of mastering the haircut itself. It is not, alas, to be a simple bob; not enough oriental blood in Miss Cooper for that.

Richard tells me to forget everything I have learnt so far and discard straight lines and geometry. 'You've only been cutting the length; now you're moving inside the haircut.' This means nothing to me and I ask for clarification.

'You have to imagine the hairs standing upright like a row of tentpoles. Cut off the top couple of inches and then push them over like dominoes. That's what you do with *this* haircut. You get a layered effect, see?'

No, I don't.

As regards the persuasion, I am armed by Sassoon's with several buzz-words or phrases that have stood the test of time and, like an encyclopaedia-salesman's professional patter, will do me proud when I meet Ms Cooper. They are as follows:

'Your hair's lovely, we can do something really exciting with it.'

'No, I won't take too much off. What I'll do is take half

of it away, but you'll look as thought you've got twice as much.'

'It's no trouble to look after.'

And if all else fails: 'It's a much younger haircut . . .' this one to be phrased in such a way as to avoid any implication that mutton is about to be dressed as lamb.

I meet Jilly Cooper at her home. This, I am told, will be a mistake. As bank managers are eunuchs if not peering over their own desks, so are hairdressers outside their salons.

'I don't want to look like mutton dressed as lamb,' are almost her first words, and my major strategic weapon is defused. I work my way through the others. A photograph of the end result will, I hope, clinch it and this is what I produce next. I was told later that this was also a mistake, since people who want to look like models in photographs can never divorce the hair from the total look and think it's a face-cut rather than a haircut you're going to give them.

The model in my picture is wearing a classic 'shake', which is what this particular haircut is called. It derives its name from the way in which the cut is given its final dressing; you ask the lady to shake her head and that is it. Dogs have been doing it for years, Sassoon's have made it fashionable.

The picture passes between Jilly and husband Leo. This too is a mistake, for he sees nothing other than the model's pouting expanse of lip and requests that to be included in the 'new look'. He also sees the tumbling cascade of fine blonde hair teasingly wrapping itself over the eyes, and the irresistible invitation so evident in them. I promise to do all this for his wife, a promise that my present skills render me entirely unable to deliver. I shake at the thought of the shake.

'Don't worry, darling,' cries Jilly as we part, 'do what you like. It will grow again.'

She's a member of the 'don't cares' . . . I shake even more.

It is difficult to describe the process of cutting a 'shake'.

It is like trying to explain why a breeze sends a ripple through a cornfield, why the random scattering of the sand can make the smoothest of beaches; it is nature turning chaos into beauty or, in this case, me turning disorder into shape. How it works, I do not know. All I can tell you is that is is hard on the fingers. Instead of gently taking each section, combing lightly through it and allowing it to fall naturally against the head as in the bob, here chunks of hair are grasped and pulled, then cut and more hair grabbed, brought into line with the last lot and cut again. Then you grab a handful the other way, then back again, and then from the back forward and from the front backwards. It's enough to make you pull your own hair out. I've heard talk before of the 'learning block', when you can go so far and no further, and I am now up against it. The hairdressing career has hit the buffers. My principle of doing exactly what I am told cannot work here; judgement is called for. Richard is tearing his hair out too.

So we turn to the block – an artificial head of hair on a dour, sour-looking plastic face, but at least it doesn't complain. Here I can pull and twist hair to my own satisfaction and resolve my own exasperations on this poor dummy. The nylon hair is thicker than human hair, and so it comes as no surprise when I have to exert rather more pressure on the scissors to cut through it – until I discover that the resistance was my fleshy palm and not the hair at all. Blood flows. If any haircut was going to draw blood it was going to be this one.

Surely, but rather slowly, I am making progress. I have been watching my fellow students closely and seeing how they bend their bodies to each movement of the comb, how they do not simply raise the scissors but make a broad upward sweep with their arms. They tease their fingers through the hair, dancing round the chair as they do it; not stooping and shuffling and straining and grunting as I do, slowly moving from side to side cursing each cut. So I try it with a flourish and, looking more like a hairdresser, I feel more like a hairdresser and, what's more I cut like a hairdresser. I am once again on an upward learning curve.

Let us hope that Ms Cooper's arrival at the salon will coincide with its peak.

The arena in which boy David will cut Lady Goliath's hair is in fashionable Sloane Street. Having never cut hair in a salon before, only in a school, it all takes me a bit by surprise. The chairs are high enough for one thing. I've just had three months of stooping over the souped-up stools you have to endure in the school, and I'm not sure I know how to cut hair without a dull ache in the back. Eyes are watching but, cleverly, no one is actually looking.

Taking advantage of the new-found luxury of the smart salon, I put my foot on the chair's hydraulic lift. I start to pump the lady up. Simultaneously, she starts to wind me up.

As I suspected, Jilly Cooper's indifference towards the end result is overtaken by intense questioning as to the final length. What is it with women? Why do they all seem to think that I shall not be happy till they are shorn like sheep? Can they really believe that it is more fun to cut six inches off a plank of wood than two? Out comes the old record: 'only a couple of inches . . . only a couple . . .' Thereafter she is well-behaved, and minutes of silence interrupt torrents of nervous chatter. I am now dancing round the chair, floating like a butterfly, stinging with my scissors like a bee. It is like a tune played on a piano the first time, all the notes are falling into the right order. Jilly's hair and I are making music. Two fingers grasp and clench a section of hair with one smooth upwards movement where before a comb and fist would have been called in to help, each slice with the scissors is now done with enough flourish to make each cut a balletic movement in itself.

'It's a wonderful cut,' mutters Jilly.

'It's a wonderful cut,' mutters Richard.

I progress through the hair in ordered fashion, regretting slightly the fact that, having at last learned to march, I am on my last parade.

I wish there could be a happy end to this tale, a completely happy end with none of the nagging doubts that linger in my mind. I want us all to end up happy at the end of the day. Sure enough, Richard is happy, delighted even. As for the other stylists, who have feigned total indifference to my performance while contriving not to miss one single move, they are impressed too. And I'm happy. Happy to be home and dry at the end of a marathon, happy to have achieved a haircut that will stand out head and shoulders above any done by anyone with experience as meagre as mine. But I shall not be totally happy till Jilly is totally happy, and I know that she is not.

Blowdrying the 'shake' is not like the 'bob', where smooth strokes of the brush under the heat of the dryer mould the hair to the shape of the head. Drying the shake is more like drying a sodden sheepdog with fingers ruffling the hair in a stream of warm air and finally bending the lady over till her head is halfway between her knees and her hair falling in a confused way over face, eyes and ears. With the dryer blowing upwards, the hair gets its final blast. Then, rather like the climax to a magic trick, you ask her to shake her head and fling it upwards and backwards. What you have is the finished cut.

This Jilly does. As she rises to see her new self in the mirror for the first time, there are two things about her face that are quite distinct. The first is the beetroot colour, due to having endured a couple of kilowatts of hot air on it for the last ten minutes. But behind it is an unmistakable disappointment.

'It's a beautiful cut . . . it's . . . I think . . . you've done very well.' It is said in the tone of an anxious parent reading a school report that is not quite up to expectations. All the right words are coming out, but she never says she likes it. 'You're brilliant, you really are. You are so clever to have done it . . .'

Very polite. Very disappointed.

The emergency services gather round, sensing, if not a full-scale disaster, then a minor incident. Richard does his best to reassure the 'lady'. 'It's really good, it makes you look good,' he swears to her. And, 'You can't tell her it makes her fifteen years younger, but it does,' he whispers to me.

The ending is not unlike the closing scene of a very dignified affair. This head of hair has occupied my entire mind for months, and it is now walking out of my life. It is a very polite farewell; we hardly exchange a word. I thank her for being so patient, she thanks me too and says it's a very good cut. She never says she likes it.

So was it a disaster or not? To me, undoubtedly. If you can't make the woman happy, what's the point? I've had a taste of the power now. In endless training sessions I have transformed scruffy-headed lasses into presentable girls who can walk out on to Bond Street, head held high. I've seen the pleasure a good haircut can bring, what an hour in a stylist's chair can do for a woman, how the skilled use of the scissors can roll back the years.

Hang on, is this *me* talking? Is this the person who just weeks ago cut hair by the rule book and saw each new head that came before me as nothing more than a chore? I am getting too close to this business. Close enough already to realise that Vidal Sassoon is right after all. I met him briefly, one of the few students in the school who ever has. At the time I sneered at his inflated view of his own profession. He told me:

'You have in your hands the power to make a woman cry for a month or make her happy for the rest of her life.'

I'm beginning to think he was right. Perhaps a few more lessons and I might have crowned Jilly's head with eternal happiness. We shall never know now. As she left, her fingers were already playing it into the old shape. Castles in the sand.

Caine
and
Able

Caine and Able

I'm afraid of actors. Always have been. Prejudiced? Perhaps, but I have met them, worked for them and, finally, attempted to become one.

If a shrink were to question me, I might say that it all stems from an early age; and if he delved further, I might be able to pin it down to row G of the Lyceum Theatre, Sheffield, *Babes in the Wood*, nineteen-fifty-something. There you would have found a terror-stricken child, palms sweating, fingers playing nervously with the shiny snake-shaped buckle on his too-tight belt, pride of the Christmas stocking.

And the fear? The man on the stage. God knows who he was or what part he was playing, but his big stick was pointing at our row and moving relentlessly in my direction. It was one of those participation games where children are invited (or dragged, in most cases) on to the stage to take part in a magic trick or sing a song or do a dance, presumably to give the rest of the cast a breather. The big gnarled stick pointed directly at me. The opportunity to play the blue toothbrush in the famous duet with a pink one, was mine. I squirmed, I slid, I rolled up hedgehog-like till I could shuffle off the seat and on to the floor.

'He's shy,' declared the man on the stage.

'He's shy,' added my Auntie Hilda, helpfully.

A liquorice allsort was thrust down into my hand from the sympathetic lady on the other side. I stayed hidden down between the rows till I was off the hook.

Now, you can put all that down to the reluctance of a seven-year-old if you like, but I knew that was not the real reason. I could have put as much into the blue toothbrush role as any Pavarotti. I could even read. I would have had

no trouble following the little ball that bounced from word
to word across the screen at the back of the stage. None of
that was a problem – it was the actor that worried me. I
didn't trust him. Why did he really want me up there and
what would he do when he'd got me? What trick did he
have up his baggy sleeve? Wasn't that stick-on red nose
merely a front for some sinister intent? I was genuinely
afraid of him.

I was afraid of Dame Edith Evans too. Just turned
nineteen and a university education in the sciences just
turned down, I had an overwhelming desire to become a
television technician. I also had total colour blindness, not
good for a engineer in an age when the Black and White
Minstrels were about to become a thing of the past. So I
had to settle for next best, and that was a job in the
theatre. Colour vision was not a problem here. As long as
you were half-blind to the miserly pay at the end of the
week, you could go far. I worked for a brief spell at the
Birmingham repertory theatre as what was called a 'stage
dayman' but really meant a stage morning, noon, and
night man.

Carpentry was one of the jobs I had to do, and it all
went rather well till the head 'chippie' found that on one
particular evening he was not able to unwrap his hand
from around his native glass of Guinness, and I was left to
build the staircase that allowed the Princess to enter from
below the stage at the climax of the Christmas play. They
seemed good stairs to me, and nobody else could find a
bad word to say about them. A bit steep, I might agree,
and perhaps not very even, but recognisable as stairs by
anybody. Then the actress tried them. What is it about
actors and actresses that exempts them from putting themselves out to help you? Why didn't this girl, who thought
the stairs impossible to climb, simply do what anyone else
would have done and make more effort? Actors!

In the end she made her grand entrance down a flight of
stairs which the drunken chippie had built. A few blows
from his trembling hammer and a few wavy cuts from his
saw were judged to result in a safer structure.

Which brings me to my confrontation with Dame Edith Evans. When you are the lighting operator, as I became at Bernard Miles's Mermaid Theatre, and your sole purpose is to illuminate the actors, it could be considered incompetent to leave a great old lady of the theatre tottering around the stage in pitch darkness, trying to deliver a moving climactic line, while you fumble backstage for your switches amidst a self-created all-enveloping gloom. And that is what I did, aged nineteen and sweating.

After sufficient light had been shed upon the Dame to allow her to bring the play to its conclusion, I felt an apology was called for. I went to her dressing-room door, took a deep breath and knocked a hesitant knock, timid as any footman taking the Queen her morning tea for the first time.

'You seem to be an incompetent young man,' she said, eyes narrowed like slits in an armoured pill box. I recoiled.

'I shall speak to Mr Miles tomorrow,' she added. The brief audience was over.

She did speak to Mr Miles and he did speak to me.

'Wear a different shirt, keep your distance, and she'll never know it's you!' was his advice.

When the BBC finally came to realise that colour vision in no way hindered the work of a sound man, they gave me a job as an assistant recordist who travelled with film crews and whose job was to hold the microphone before the players. Sometimes they were politicians, commentators or ordinary folk, but when they were actors, more often than not a pleasant enough job turned sour.

Technicians have a word for actors; they call them the 'talent'. 'Let's have the talent on the set,' they will sneer. Or, 'Quiet please, the talent is learning its lines,' if they really want to make them feel at home. There is no doubt about it, technicians and actors are rarely on the same side.

Television presenters, on the other hand, seem to be somewhere in the middle. Whereas an actor might only make an occasional TV appearance, regular presenters know that programmes made with grudging technicians are programmes hardly worth making. TV people need technicians like cows need milking – they provide the daily flow. Cross them and it can get painful. But when TV man meets actor, watch out for sparks; for while the actor has perfected the art of being someone else, the television man is being himself and so, in the company of actors feels as though he is at a party where everyone is in fancy dress but him. Uncomfortable.

So I am in a difficult position. I am a turncoat – a technician, turned presenter, who is about to become an actor.

If you measure it by the yard, my task is a fairly slender one. I am to prepare for a role in a feature film alongside Michael Caine. This sounds grand, but when the sum total of your lines is less than a hundred words you will see why it hardly seems worth booking a ticket at the next Oscar ceremony.

I am hardly equipped for this part. It calls for a ruthless soldier, a mercenary with such awesome force of evil personality that he could wither a leg with one look. He was once described to me as a brute who 'only smiled when strangling kittens'. He's also German, which will require me to perfect some accent or other, and during the course of the blink-and-you'll-miss-it scene, this chap gives Caine a fist in the stomach. So I must acquire an aura of intimidation, make women and children run screaming in fear. There is an accent to master, a cross between an old recording of a Hitler rally and something out of *Dad's Army*, and I must learn how to restrain myself when it comes to embedding my clenched fist in the multi-million-dollar Caine stomach. As small parts go, this is quite a big one.

I suspect I'm a bit too nice for it, which could be a problem. My tutor, Malcolm, tells me that to play evil you've got to *be* a bit evil. Strange job this man has, bringing out the worst in people. If he had a shop, his neon sign would proclaim 'Find a new and vicious you!' His theatre of operation is in the basement of the theatre of the young hopefuls at RADA, the Royal Academy of Dramatic Art – or Drastic Art in my case since it is clear from the look on Malcolm's face that he believes my chances of becoming a villain match those of Andy Pandy mugging Looby Loo.

Malcolm has brought his support team to help: about a dozen young actors, some unshaven and stubbly (judging from their ages wine-growers would probably class this a first growth), the girls with short cropped hair, convict-style. They have enough rings in their ears, boys and girls, to hold up a good-sized pair of curtains. And here I stand, in my Viyella shirt and conspicuous new jeans, alongside Malcolm, captivated by the slightly enlarged and rubbery nature of his lips and wondering what will be done to me, by whom and with what?

They call this the improvisation class.

The room is black and dimly lit, Malcolm's jacket is black and so too is his hair. All I see is a face, and those lips. They flex.

'Go and sit on that chair,' he orders.

I run towards it. There's a girl on it, dressed in black again. Only the cropped blonde hair and round, moony face is visible.

I am suspicious. I ask her to move. She says nothing and moves not an inch. I ask again. Nowt. And again.

'Why?' she eventually utters.

'I want to sit on it because he told me to,' I reply, mildly mannered, like a curate insisting on his place in the pew.

'He told you to, and that's the reason you're going to push me off my seat?' she snarls and crosses her legs, raising her skirt slightly too far above the knee to have, any longer, the look of a wronged woman. This does not impress Malcolm, who is clearly looking for a violent climax to this little scene. So I decide to play my own game rather than his. I may never go down in theatrical history as the great aggressor but I'm running for 'most promising persuader of the year'.

'I'm asking you in a perfectly reasonable manner if I

can sit on that chair, now what right do you have to occupy it?'

My argument is abruptly halted. Malcolm is despairing. Those lips are curling up at the corners a little.

He changes tack.

'I want you to do exactly as she says,' he screams. I sense rising anger. Not mine, alas. The girl gets up from the chair to deliver her orders. If I was feeling cheeky enough, I'd go and sit on that chair, but I'll play a little longer.

'Run on the spot . . . knees up . . . *up* . . . *up*. Touch your toes . . . *bend* . . .' she shouts.

I do as much as I am physically able. Then the crowd join in.

'*Bend* . . . *run* . . . *jump*,' they all shout from out of the blackness.

'Get on the floor,' commands the hard-as-nails blonde.

I'm down there before the words leave her lips. Malcolm throws in the towel.

'Looking at you,' he sums up, 'I see a man who will refuse to say no, but not a man who will go out and say, "I want." I want to turn your anger round, I want to turn it into aggression. At the moment, it's all defence.'

I'm really not playing hard to get. There's no anger in me. Not the sort that forces women off chairs, anyway.

Malcolm changes tack again.

'I want you to be a mobster, ruthless leader of a gang. Kathy can be your moll. All the others are members of your gang. They have got suspicions that you've run off with the loot from the last bank raid and they want to get rid of you and take charge themselves. Now, by voice, by threat, you've got to show them who is the boss.'

This appeals to me. I'm on the defence. If Malcolm's got me summed up, this should be easy. I go for the weediest-looking one, the one with combed hair and wearing the pressed shirt. I grab him by the collar and pull him towards me. Our noses nearly touch.

'Who's the boss, answer me that . . . *tell me* . . . you little rat,' and on I go, spewing out lines first read in

American comics of the 1950s. 'Who taught you everything you know?' I snarl as I move my hands to his throat, taking rather more pleasure in this than Malcolm intended. The boy looks worried, or is he acting? Worried, I think. The leopard is changing his spots.

The stark, hitherto immobile blonde comes at me. I'm there first and repel her with a well-placed blow to the shoulder. She looks worried too.

All the old gangster scenes from *Dixon of Dock Green* are flooding back. I go round each of my gang, raising their faces to mine with a rude flick of a finger under their chins, promising certain extinction if they do not swear their allegiance. My blood is boiling. Lip from any of them and I'll beat them to pulp there and then. But Malcolm calls time. He's worried now.

As I smear the sweat across my brow, wipe away the dribble from my frothing lips and cool my newly released anger, Malcolm congratulates me on a fine performance. Only one problem – that was no performance, that was just a shouting match. If that's all there is to being a bad boy of the silver screen, then every soccer hooligan in the country would be on a fat Hollywood contract. I don't feel this is the whole story. Did Marlon Brando have to throw girls off chairs to show his authority? Did Bogart threaten Sam with removal from the piano stool if he didn't play it again? Shouters and screamers are weak men.

Take then this figure, whose only theatrical experience has been at the hands of the apprentice spear-carriers of RADA, who has shown himself to be a man of such stature that he kissed the floor when ordered by a fierce girl with a cropped haircut, who has so little natural ruthlessness when it comes to displacing persons from chairs that if he were ever to be appointed a traffic warden he would cry over every ticket, whose only armour consists of the odd line from a few old TV police soaps and whose major problem is keeping a straight face.

Take him and place him at the foot of a winding gravel drive that leads to an ancient Surrey farmhouse. Watch him twitch as each reluctant step takes him nearer the door.

There's a rhinoceros on the left! Glass-fibre, of course, although such a wild and lumbering beast as this would not seem out of place stalking the grounds of this man's home. There is a legend about this life-size rhino (who is, I am told, called Hornby either because of the nature of his vicious tusk or the general off-the-rails life of his owner). The story goes that one drunken night a group of high-spirited lads came up from the village, took the plastic creature and liberated him in the pub car park. Word was quickly sent to his owner that this kidnap had taken place. The reaction was swift. Angered at the loss of Hornby (a gift from hell-raiser and drum-destroyer Keith Moon), he took out a kilt and wrapped it round him. Down his knee-high plaid stockings he thrust a sharpened steel dirk and, with half a dozen men similarly dressed, he marched upon the village. The villagers' reaction was just as swift. Experience told them that this assault was unlikely to be a tongue-in-cheek affair.

Windows were boarded, the pub closed an hour early and the landlord left town for the night.

Gossip surely? What do I have to fear from a man with such a reputation? He's an actor. I expect he was just improvising on a rather grand scale. Malcolm would have approved.

I knock on the door. It opens fast enough to create a draught. Short cowboy boots are just visible beneath the hem of a long, grey army greatcoat. Underneath, a red and white striped rugby shirt. The face looks as though it has not seen a razor for three days and the hand that is not crushing the door handle is firmly holding on to a half pint mug. It looked as though it might be a vodka and tonic – not the first of the day but more likely the last of the night before.

'Come in, Paul,' he whispers with a deep, coarse voice.

'Thank you, Mr Reed,' I reply with a shallow, dry-to-the-point-of-cracking voice and walk in, thankfully avoid-ing what I expected to be his pulverising handshake. This must be how toreadors feel the first time they let the bull out. This is Oliver Reed.

His room is a surprise. Beams and brass and white paint. Clean and ordered. Not the sort of place to swing an empty gin bottle. Not the ideal stage for a bull-in-a-china-shop performance.

'Come through to the play room,' he invites. I wonder what he means by play?

We go to a barn at the back of the house. Not far, so we don't have to exchange a word. A full-sized snooker table dominates; crumbling furniture fills the space around it – cheap, jumble sale furniture, unlike the polished and preserved antiques of the house. Through an arched door at the end of the long room is the bar, the altar at the head of this chapel built as a monument to green baize and distilleries.

We sit down. He's rather charming. Even through the crazed glass of the wire-rimmed spectacles there's warmth. This is not yet the confrontation that I had feared. This is like burly old pals at the rugby club: polite, civilised, but never far from a drink.

'A dangerous man has a great silence about him,' he offers, and then says nothing, proving his point. His eyes don't move much either, nor does he blink. I try a nervous smile.

'Don't blink,' he says with no stress on either word.

'On a cinema screen, your eye is six feet wide. Start blinking like Bambi – what are the audience going to think. Will they think you're deadly? You don't see a cobra blink, do you?' His voice rises a little towards the end of his sentence. The eyelids are still unmoving.

'No,' I reply, just holding back a 'sir'.

'Rehearse in the bathroom, then try it out in the pub. Just look at someone and don't blink and see how uncomfortable they get.'

I move uneasily in the chair, blinking like hell.

'Straighten your hair,' he barks. 'Villains have straight hair, not curly hair. Don't use your eyebrows. Keep them still.'

The old straight face problem overtakes me again. I sit still, unblinking, waxwork-like, then I crack up.

'Don't smile. You're a villain!'

'Remember,' he goes on, winding himself up like a storm brewing, 'villains never get surprised, they just handle situations. So if you're a villain and you want to look surprised, you just . . . do . . . that.'

He raises one eyebrow. Not far, quarter of an inch at the most, but devastating. His eyelids haven't flickered for at least half a minute; mine are up and down like chattering teeth.

'And then whisper your line,' he adds. 'Remember the whispering giant. The sound man will tell you he's got lots of background noise and can't hear you. You say to him, "Look, I've come three thousand miles to play this part, you get it!" The sound man will look stern, but you look him in the eye, keep your mouth shut and don't blink.'

Now comes the bit I'm dreading.

'I want to hear your lines,' says Reed sternly, staring me in the eye. I delve into my back pocket for a crumpled piece of paper with my words on them. I feel like a new boy at school producing lines for the sixth-form bully.

I've picked some lines from the script. They're not the lines I shall have to do in my screen role, but similar. It's a middle-European thug, with a bit of menace about him. The lines go: 'I told you, old man, to leave us alone. You're going to get the young lady in trouble, but not half as much trouble as you're going to get yourself.'

In my approach to the interpretation of this particular role I have in my mind my German O-level classes, which I decide will do fine for the accent, and after all that Malcolm has taught me I feel a raised voice might carry the part better. Eyes blinking as fast as my racing pulse, I shout them out at Reed.

'I tolt you olt marn tu leef uz alorn!'

He says nothing, for a long time. Then: 'I beg your pardon? Are you serious? You're shouting because you've been to RADA and the sound man has told you to speak up. I told you to speak softly if you want to be deadly,' he says softly, very deadly.

'And what's all that with the mouth,' and he twists his lips, imitating me. 'Are you trying to kiss me? Forget the bloody stupid accent. Just do the "I tolt . . ." it doesn't need any more. Eyes fixed. Hair straight. Now do it.'

'I tolt you . . .' my eyes are glued to his; looks can kill, and this one of mine might just inflict a minor flesh wound '. . . old man to leave us . . .' I'm whispering '. . . alone.'

'Much better,' says Reed, 'now do the rest.'

I look down at my piece of dog-eared paper.

'Why are you reading, you've only got three fucking lines and you can't remember them!' I open my mouth, half hoping an excuse might come out.

'I know you've got three things to remember, eyes fixed, voice down and your lines, but my God,' sighs Reed loudly.

Then I try my next line on him, which goes, 'What are you fools doing in here? Get him . . . *get him*.' It comes out, 'Vot are yoo fullz doink in ere? Get him . . . *get him*.'

'Vot's with all this vot?' asks Reed. 'You're supposed to be middle European, they don't say *vot*, nobody says *vot* except, perhaps, German generals. And don't shout,' he shouts. 'Play against it, bark it . . . *bark it*.'

Like a schoolteacher at the end of his tether, like a sergeant major whose troop cannot put one step before the other, like the conductor whose orchestra is out of tune, Reed snaps. He rises from his leather chair and heads in my direction. No problem here. Malcolm prepared me for this. It's all one big improvisation. Reed thunders towards me and I feel the expanse of his rough hand on my neck. Is it improvisation hell! I try to laugh as if to say, gosh what a good joke this is, Ollie. Ollie meanwhile is moving relentlessly towards the door, dragging me behind like a caveman might have dragged his spouse. He slings me out. Thank God he opened the door first.

He leaves me out in the cool, fresh air just long enough to be wondering if he really meant it. Then the door opens and there once again is that warm, gentle man who opened the door to me a mere couple of hours earlier, although by now it feels like a week. Inevitably, he offers me a drink and some good advice, not about acting, but about the power game that actors play.

'Most actors are insecure,' he tells me. 'The best way to handle them is to use the tricks I've taught you. Look them in the eye, keep your voice down and call them 'sir' and don't mean it – and make sure they know you don't mean it. Film-making is a slow business; an American actor once taught me, very early on, that the best thing to do was to learn to sleep during the day. You might have only one line to do that day and it might be at the end of the day, so make love at night, keep your nights very busy, lots of wine, lots of ladies, lots of cakies, and when you go to your dressing-room, sleep.'

Then he pauses. His eyes glaze a little and the cobra look comes over his face.

'You probably won't get a dressing-room,' he says, 'three-liners don't. You'll probably be out there with the cattle and the cows at the bottom of the field.'

On my way home I try hard to remember his lessons. I glaze my eyes, freeze my eyelids, whisper like a giant. At the bottom of the drive, I meet Hornby once again. He's the only animal I feel safe with round here.

Unfortunately, my part in this film is not a foregone conclusion. The acting profession still has another humiliation to throw at me before I can enter the club and get on with being a baddie.

I've got to pass the audition – impress the writers and directors that I have it in me to be a mean man. I failed with RADA, I don't think Oliver Reed gives much for my chances, and as I make my way to Shepperton studios I feel very fourth division; something spectacular will have to be pulled from the bag if relegation is to be avoided.

Shepperton is the birthplace of some of the finest celluloid ever to come out of a film studio but, symbolically of the British film industry, the paint is beginning to peel and the edges are fraying. Where great actors once intoned, they now build house-size replicas of soap powder packets to film tricksy commercials.

It's rather like an army camp. All the buildings look temporary, a bit government-surplus. Take down the old movie posters, replace them with aeromaps and you could run World War Two from here. Staircases are wooden, with green paint generously applied, slapped on by careless squaddies no doubt. The bunker I'm looking for is the one marked *Water*; that's the unlikely name of the film in which I hope to make my cinema début.

Although I've read the script, there's not a lot I know about this film except that it's supposed to be a comedy, I think. Jokes on paper have never worked for me, but it's written by Dick Clement and Ian La Frenais, writers of hit TV series such as *The Likely Lads* and *Auf Wiedersehen, Pet*. I announce myself at the rather small office and take the only seat, which is a box. In the office next door, an American barks down a phone, something about getting an oil rig to the West Indies. He gets cut off and asks the girl in the office I'm sitting in to re-dial for him. It's a Stoke-on-Trent number. Before barking recommences he closes the door on me. Quite right. Careless talk costs lives.

Dick Clement comes in and looks around. We *had* met some months before when a part for me in his film was first mooted, but there is no flicker of recognition in his face. Probably thinks I'm another bloody extra on the scrounge.

He's back in his room when I'm called in to meet him and La Frenais. Both are sitting on a low leather couch, both in jeans, both in blue shirts and blue guernseys. Very close, this partnership.

Clement outlines the plot of the film, which doesn't interest me much since all I have to do is get my lines right. They are as follows:

KESSLER: (Looking down at stopwatch) Four minutes and sixteen seconds. Then they rendezvous with the yacht and we are in Martinique before dawn.

WOMAN: You have done well, Kessler. I congratulate you!

KESSLER: Hand-picked mercenaries, the scum of the earth.

Then there's the big scene, the one opposite Michael Caine. That goes:

CAINE: Who are you? Why are you here?

KESSLER: For the bloodshed and the money. We are the dogs of war.

Not a lot, set against Hamlet, but I'm confident of being able to learn the lines.

Clement makes all the running; La Frenais says little, but it's sharp when it comes.

'Have you thought about the character? What is Kessler like?'

'Arrogant,' I reply, 'stiff, upright, always at attention. The sort of soldier who always thinks he's right.'

'I was thinking more about his haircut,' says Clement. 'I want you to look brutal.'

'Less like an amiable schoolteacher from Belsize Park,' slings in La Frenais, looking at me worriedly.

'How tall are you?' asks Clement.

'Six foot one.'

'Good. You're bigger than Caine.' My only plus point so far.

They start discussing me like two doctors over a corpse.

'I think he needs a scar.'

'Yes, a big one,' adds La Frenais, smirking.

'We could shave his head bald,' says Clement.

I'm curious now. How much of this eventual character Kessler is going to be the result of my unblinking, whispering, threatening efforts, and how much will be thanks to a plastic scar and electric hair-clippers?

'Fifty-two per cent make-up, the rest is you!' says Clement.

He's just halved the task.

Clement asks me to read the scene on the beach. This is

where Kessler, ruthless leader of mercenaries, is explaining to the rich moll who has hired him how his plan will work. He's showing her how good his men are at scaling cliffs. Hence, 'Four minutes and sixteen seconds, then they rendezvous with the yacht . . . etc.'

I stand in front of both of them, about six feet away. Like an electric kettle, it's all boiling up inside me. I stare them full in the face, my eyes welded in the open position. I give it the German accent:

'Four minuts unt zixteen zeconts,' then I pause, for dramatic effect. I'm freezing the blood in their veins, I can feel it, draining the life-force from their bodies with this reading. I can hear children bursting into tears as my fearsome aura spreads. Old ladies are hastily sliding bolts across their back doors.

'Zen zeh rendezvous wiz ze yot.' I pause to let the full depth of my interpretation dawn upon them, then I go on, 'Unt ve are bek in Martinique.' I pause, take a shallow breath to heighten the tension, then deliver the final phrase, 'Before dorn.' I'm drained.

'Too slow,' says Clement, and rattles it off like a child doing its two-times table. There's no art in that. He asks me to do it again, but faster. Still with eyes fixed, blood-chilling expression and in a whisper, I go at it like a bull.

'Much better,' says Clement.

Then I ask, 'Was I brutal enough for you?' La Frenais sniggers at my 'did the earth move for you?' line of questioning.

'Think like a mugger,' advises Clement. 'Think like a man who would barbecue his own granny,' adds La Frenais.

The poor old hall mirror is taking the brunt of my experimentations. A snarl hits it every time I pass, a grimace, a withering look. At least I hope that's how they're turning out; it's just the same old face to me. I long for jowls pendulous enough to reach my knees, ravine-like creases in my skin, piercing eyes that shrivel old ladies, a stare that sends rats back down holes.

But I don't see any of that. Just the amiable school-teacher look, and lines that sound as though he's trying to learn a few phrases to take on a school trip to Bavaria.

'Four zer blutshid,' snarl, grate of teeth, 'unt zerr munay.' The cats flee at this terrible grumbling around their house. All comers are now greeted with an unblinking look. I stare at them. Breadman, postman, milkman, the lot. The children cry when they see me.

'You've got red eyes, dear,' says a neighbour. 'Have you had a cold?' She is unmoved. So are the rest of them.

'You can't be a villain with curly hair,' said Oliver Reed. I am considering Brylcreem.

Then there's the walk. This seems hardly convincing either. I'm watching all those TV documentaries about the parachute regiment, the SAS, the Special Boat Squadron. Few of them seem to be knock-kneed like me, but perhaps if I'm lucky I'll be able to do all my lines standing still. It occurs to me that too few lines can be as difficult as too many. They become too important to be lost, for to miss is to blow the whole part. A misplaced phrase amongst a thousand is not going to damage any actor's Oscar chances, but when you've only got a handful of words, every single one has to be considered and weighed and delivered.

So consider my most important line, the one I shall have to deliver to Michael Caine: 'For the blood shed, and the money. We are the dogs of war.'

Do I draw it out for all it's worth, make the camera linger on me for as long as possible? Give it impact? Roll it round the mouth to make every word last as long as half a dozen? Do a Donald Sinden on it?

It might go, 'For the bloodshed . . .' whispered, but powerfully, and then a pause to allow Caine's blood to chill, then unleash myself like a coiled spring for a scream, '. . . and the *money*.' Maintain this crescendo through another good long pause for the audience to weigh the plot and realise the full importance of this character (always assuming he has any importance – I have only read my lines so far, nobody else's) Then, like a Wembley crowd on a high, another scream, '*We are the dogs of war!*'

Or there's the other approach: the Bogart touch, what Oliver Reed called the whispering giant. If only the mirror could speak.

There's a long journey to the location. I travel light. The only concession to my new-found career is a multi-coloured, striped robe – the sort you see actors drape around themselves as they lean back in folding chairs and complain about backstage at the National, retelling for the umpteenth time what Larry said to them twenty years ago and eyeing the make-up girl (or the wardrobe boy).

At least the journey gives me a chance to read the script. It takes surprisingly little time. There aren't many words to a page, not spoken words anyway. There are lots of 'enters looking harassed and kicks over a table as he makes his way towards . . . etc.', but as far as actual dialogue goes, I get through the lot in about an hour. I eagerly scan every new page, looking for my grand entrance.

The story is set on a Caribbean island called Cascara, a British-owned island where the pot-smoking Governor is played by Michael Caine. Recent explorations have failed to find any oil and the island is on its uppers. Caine appeals to the British government for help. They send out a man from the Foreign Office (Leonard Rossiter) who, instead of bringing good news, tells Caine that Britain has washed its hands of Cascara. Then the oil rig blows, but instead of a sticky flow of oil it emits a fountain of fizzy mineral water – Perrier. Cascara now takes on a new international importance and Britain wants it back. The Americans are interested, and the French want to gain control so their own precious mineral-water market is not threatened. I am the ruthless mercenary hired by the French to regain control of the island. I've got about six lines to do it.

On my way to this Caribbean location, feeling warmer with every mile, I look out of the train window. Why does it say Newton Abbot, and why am I changing on to the branch line to Barnstaple? Remember the American on the phone to Stoke-on-Trent? It seems that Michael Caine is not the only thing of enormous stature in this movie; there's a real oil rig, and to take it from the Midlands to north Devon is reasonable, but across the Atlantic is just a bit too far, even for a feature film with a multi-million-dollar budget.

The road to Hartland Point takes you through the high-hedged lanes of North Devon, gaps providing occasional glimpses of the sea. From the top of a rise you get a tantalising view of Lundy Island some ten miles offshore. It is the very essence of the English countryside: cows graze on succulent green grass. Stone-built farmhouses litter the scene, trees bend in submission to the westerly winds that lash this rocky and exposed coast. But two miles further down the rocky lane, as obvious as a boil on a baby's bottom, as unlikely as a blemish on a well-cut diamond, stands an ugly, greasy oil rig. It is a credit to whichever creative arm of this operation placed it here, for it looks as though it's been here for years.

You don't have to be a geologist to spot that there's something wrong underfoot. When all around is exposed rocks and craggy outcrops and you find your foot is falling on bright yellow sand, you begin to suspect. You don't need a diploma in forestry to know that not many palm trees grow in Devon, yet here they are, swaying gently. Only the grating sound of the fibre-glass leaves distinguishes them from the creaking of the real ones.

A bronzed team of labourers, lighting men, props men, wardrobe and make-up – all just back from the Caribbean – are heaving their tanned frames around, shouting into walkie-talkies, getting ready for some activity.

But what? There's no camera here, the stars aren't due until tomorrow. As far as cast goes, there's only me, and I've been moved on twice to make way for a lorry-load of plastic bushes, replicas of West Indian flora. And all because this oil rig gets home-sick when more than a day's journey away from Stoke-on-Trent. That's why although the majority of this film has been shot under the heat of the Caribbean sun, the bits that I'm in, and a few more, are at the mercy of the Hartland Point climate. As a faint mist rolls in from the sea and thickens as it meets the land, shrouding the palm trees in an unaccustomed fog, I wonder how long I shall be here before my handful of lines are committed to celluloid.

The next day, I'm on the scene at 8 am sharp as the call sheet ordered. The call sheet is a document giving the orders for the day; it is an optimistic piece – few of its hopes and aspirations ever bear fruit. The appearance of my name on it for the first day does not necessarily mean that I shall have to do anything, nor does the absence of one's name mean anything either. But at least there's breakfast. Not a full breakfast, you understand, just a snack to keep these emaciated bodies together till the poor chap in the mobile kitchen can fry his five stone of sliced bacon. The appetiser is a catering jar of marmalade and one knife, too short to reach the bottom of the jar and not quite long enough to be reached if accidentally dropped into the pot. As this is the first day of filming, the numbers are swelling: we're up to nearly a hundred by now. They creep out of lorries, from inside caravans, from out of the false undergrowth. How many does it have to be before they bring another knife out? There's coffee as well, and that is clutched tightly between warm hands chilled by this clammy June mist.

All eyes spend at least one minute in five looking up, hoping to see the sun and finding only low cloud and mist. They haven't even got the camera out. We've only been here a quarter of an hour and the call sheet has become a fiction.

A Mercedes draws up and out gets the head boy – a Bunteresque figure with a bullying way and a withering look for any member of the crew who steps out of line. His rank is that of first assistant director, a smoother of paths for the real director, Dick Clement. The head boy's badge of office is a viewfinder he wears round his neck. It's a piece of darkened glass in a circular frame, like a monocle, and with it he can look directly at the sun and observe whether clouds are winging their way across and threatening to cast a shadow over his proceedings. He scans the sky in every direction. It's as pointless as a man wearing sunglasses in a candle-lit room; thick fog is closing in. I'm wrapping an overcoat across my short-sleeved shirt and the marmalade pot is doing good business as men and women gather sadly on the hillside. The caterer has the look of a man who is about to feed the five thousand, and the head boy is praying for a meteorological miracle. We all wait for a sign, or at least a hint from the head boy, when he's finally extracted his fist from the marmalade pot.

What do all these people do? I've appeared before cameras before, and I know how film crews work, but this one takes some believing. The trucks with costumes fill half a field on their own. There's another pantechnicon or two with all the bits they can screw on the camera to make it zoom high in the sky or scrape close to the ground. I've seen half a dozen men come out of that lorry alone, and there's one poor lad with an old horsebox full of goats who shoot out as soon as the tailgate is dropped and set about a systematic mowing of the hillside. When they find out it's free, I expect the goats will be at the marmalade too.

What blind faith these people have. The call sheet says that shots on the oil rig will be the first and so, though drizzle is turning to heavy rain, under an increasingly leaden sky, the gear moves into the pre-ordained position. Even I can tell it's a waste of time. It's clear that any shots done here will have to look as though they're done in the Caribbean, and I dare say it is crossing more minds than mine to wonder uneasily how often this rugged outcrop in the Bristol Channel is actually sundrenched. The head boy could easily spare everyone the misery of moving away from the coffee urn but, not daring to pre-empt any wish of the director, he lets us go through the charade of moving.

Another Mercedes. This time it's Clement. Black faces match darkening skies. No decision appears to be made, and Clement stalks off down a rocky roadway which leads to what was once a pretty, white-washed holiday cottage. Now it looks like a Naafi. It's become the production centre, and the dampish rooms that sheltered cliff-walkers and hikers have become dressing-rooms for the stars. Caine will get a room here – as will Leonard Rossiter and Billy Connolly – and then this little house will be full. Oliver Reed was right. 'Three-liners get put down the field with the cattle,' he'd warned. For cattle, read goats.

Some have brought a novel with them to while away the hours. I prefer the call sheet. It promises my first scene tomorrow; that's the scene on the beach where I boast to the French lady about the quality of the mercenaries I have hired. I've learnt the lines because I thought it would be too busy on location; now I find I could have memorised *Hamlet* as well. Rumour spreads like a breeze making its way across a cornfield. Eyes are on the head boy, his gestures and nods being read like the jerks of a tic-tac man on a race-course. There's a work-site hut on the oil rig and lighting men, sound men, make-up and a few more pour into it. Arc lights are beamed through the windows to give it that tropical feel and, not content with the drizzle that God has provided, the head boy decides he can do better and orders hosepipes to play on the window. A quarter of a mile away, up at the top of the hill, a truck is heard to start up. It's not any old truck, it's the catering wagon, and all on this set know the churning of its engine as if it were the wails of one of their own children. It makes its stately way down the bumpy road and stops just off the set, the driver knowing from experience where the camera is likely to be operating, and keeping clear. Out of it comes fried eggs, bacon, huge sausages, scrambled eggs, kippers and fish fingers. You are not given a choice. A bit of each is pressed between bread and you must handle it as best you can.

I have not felt so lonely since my first day at school. Few of this lot had met before but that is no barrier to their forming an instant brotherhood: united against the common foe who is strutting towards me, the new boy, his eye-piece bouncing on his gut. It's the head boy.

'Can you find Costume and get yourself fitted up. I might need you later on.'

I roam the hillside looking for the costume wagon. What's the alternative? Can I stop someone and say, 'I'm Kessler, do you know where the costume van is?'

Of course I can. I'm in this film, aren't I? Don't they call these 'supporting' roles because they bolster up the rest? No stone in the pyramid is less important than any other. I am 'the talent' now, I say to myself, but it doesn't help me find the costume wagon.

At last, in a field on its own, I find a truck bulging with uniforms, boots and helmets. Somewhere in the middle, like a rat in a haystack, is the costume designer. He clearly expects me to have done most of the designing for him.

'Have you got any ideas about the uniform?' I haven't.

'Will you carry a gun?' I don't know.

'Do you know how soldiers tie up their boots?' I don't.

He flings me a pair of combat trousers and a camouflage jacket from a pile that looks as though it has not moved since *A Bridge Too Far*.

'Keep it loose, don't do too many buttons up. I'm trying to hide that,' and he slaps the back of his hand across my midriff, sending out ripples that meet round the back.

'We can add artificial sweat under the armpits to make it look a bit steamy,' he adds. It won't be necessary.

I climb into this lot, keeping it loose. When fully dressed, I stand for the first time and look in the mirror: then look again. It's worrying. I really could be a soldier. The ankles on the boots come so high that they force your legs outwards, correcting bandiness and artificially inducing the well placed stride of a soldier. As I leave the truck, the studs on the boot make a satisfying thud as they hit the ground. I look for a sunset to walk off into.

Of course, there is no sun. That's why they're all still crowded into a little hut doing all the scenes which can be done out of the rain and aren't marred by a thick fog swirling around outside. I feel a lot more comfortable on the set now. I feel I can go and poke my nose in. The costume has been my ticket. Everyone knows exactly where

I stand: I'm the talent. No longer will I have to take my place in the coffee queue with the scene-painters and lightbulb-polishers – I'll be like the rest of the talent and get forced to the back.

There's a lot of pacing going on, much of it by Clement whose watch no longer shows minutes passed, but dollars expended. He recognises me this time.

'Like the costume, but the hair's wrong,' and he reaches out and twirls the locks that curl around my ears. 'Go and have a word with make-up.'

Once again, I'm roaming the hillside. I try the cottage this time. The door is shrouded in camouflage netting in case the small white house appears by accident in one of the shots, which might destroy the Caribbean atmosphere. The house seems very quiet. There certainly isn't any talent here – you'd hear it a mile off. In the corner of what looks like a sixth-form common room I find, slumped across a sofa, a portly young figure, his shirt open to his waist, a well tanned chest and an earring showing beneath his greased black hair. He stirs as I enter.

'I'm the dresser. I wash the stars' costume at the end of every day. Do you want me to do your socks?' he asks in a limp-wristed sort of way. 'I wash the knickers of [and here he added the name of one of the leading ladies] and do you know what I do? I spit on them and then rub them hard with Vim.' That warm relationship between talent and craftsmen is alive and well on this location.

I have to look no further, make-up finds me. The head boy has heralded my arrival by walkie-talkie. Strictly speaking, it isn't make-up, it's the hairdresser, or camp barber in my case.

'Basically you need most of it off. Not a complete shave, more of a short crewcut,' he says.

I suggest not too much, trying hard not to suggest reluctance but implying that I have given every detail of this part the most careful consideration, even down to the length of every hair.

The barber has in his hand some device which emits a

buzzing noise. I can't see it, only hear it. The buzzing gets closer.

'It wouldn't work if you just put lots of cream on and combed it close to my head?' I begged lamely. It wouldn't.

For the first time, I am really afraid. I was worried when the RADA students kicked, I was concerned when Oliver Reed lifted me by the collar, but the evil intent of this man has got them all beat. I think back to my childhood, to all the times aunties and other women have cooed over my curly hair. And behind me is this brute with a pair of shears who is going to cut away the only head of hair I have ever had.

I try to play for time, but before I can say anything I feel the cold steel on my neck. It's all too late. Sure, it will grow again, but when? And in between, how will I explain?

With one movement his clippers glide from the back of my neck across to my brow. He leaves a furrow as if a plough has passed that way. It takes only a few more strokes and it is gone. Only a little trimming left and I've got a scalp like a panscrub. It might have hurt less if he hadn't grinned with every stroke. People gather, as at the scene of an accident.

'Don't worry, you'll get over it. It actually looks quite good.'

Some even try and tell you it looks better. Better than what? Better for frightening babies perhaps, for mugging old ladies. For better or worse, I had grown accustomed to the old me, and could have wept at my loss.

Make-up was no problem after that. Brown muck was artistically applied to my face, filth painted under my fingernails, and a cruel scar struck half an inch upwards from the corner of my eye. I half expected the demon barber to come and do it with a cut-throat razor, but plastic was used instead; layer after layer painted on till it resembled a gruesome gash. That process takes about an hour and would have to be repeated every time my name appears on the call-sheet.

Mustn't be late for the head boy. I get out of the make-up chair as fast as I can and make my way down the road to the set. I go over the lines in my mind, just to be certain. It's just after four o'clock. The viewfinder bounces as Himself paces towards me. Not a word of how I look, or my hair, or even a hint in his face that might suggest I'm any different to the last time we met.

'I won't need you today, after all. Thanks,' and he was away, having caught sight of the catering truck making its way down the hill with the tea urns.

An hour's dressing, an hour's make-up, an hour's agony under the hair-clippers. And the bugger doesn't want me.

The dresser does. 'Can I wash your socks?' he enquires. He has a look in his eye that is daring me to say yes.

The days are getting a little repetitious. Eight o'clock sharp and I'm on the set. Newly found confidence makes me a force to be reckoned with round the marmalade jar. Then it's into make-up for an hour to have the scar fixed in position and checked against Polaroid photos taken on the first day. I climb into the uniform, keeping it loose and hiding my gut. Then I sit down and the rest of my day is undisturbed except by the full breakfast at ten, lunch at twelve, tea and cakes at three and sandwiches and coffee at six if filming looks like going on. As far as acting is concerned, the act of staying awake is the only performance I have to give. It goes on like this for three days. I've seen less of that camera than an extra on the back row in *Zulu*. But at least I've found a new hobby. It's a time-consuming one: I'm avoiding Billy Connolly.

Not there is anything wrong with Connolly. Far from it. He is always willing and ready to chat and can keep it up for hours. With each passing minute the dialogue edges more towards monologue, which becomes a string of jokes. All very funny ones, but after an hour the strain of laughing is greater than the pleasure derived. Through his glazed look, Billy does not spot this. Eventually he tires. Five minutes later you'll hear another outburst of guffawing from behind a lorry. Billy has moved on.

You can't help but like the man. As far as *joie de vivre* goes, this man has a double helping, and your only concern might be when he starts to get serious. Imagine a volatile Glaswegian, high on whisky and pouring out the old-pal act till one misplaced word from you turns him against you. That's when he'll punch you in the face. There's no physical violence to fear in Billy, but when he gets high on his own wit he can unleash a cruel tongue, as damaging as any broken bottle. Bad for fragile egos.

But he talks a lot of sense about the film-making business, which is in many ways a nonsense. We sit astride a plastic palm tree and I tell him how worried I am by the prospect of facing Michael Caine.

'Don't be,' he insists, telling me that this is only his second feature film, making us both beginners.

'Now if you had to go on with Michael Caine for ninety minutes, that would be something to get worried about. You act it all in little bursts and then you go for lunch.'

The feature film business gets less real the more I see of it. Behind Connolly staggers a Connolly lookalike. They could be brothers. In fact, it's a stunt man dressed and made-up to look exactly like Connolly ready to do the dangerous action scenes.

'There's no reality whatsoever involved,' says Billy. 'The real world doesn't belong in showbusiness. If it did you'd have joiners on the stage of the London Palladium making coffee tables. We're all pretending, we're playing at little doctors and nurses.'

I try my German accent for him at his request. He says it's OK, but detects my basic and as yet unresolved problem – embarrassment.

'It will be embarrassing while it lasts, but it's only for two or three minutes and then you do it again. The second time will feel better and after the third one you'll be ready for anything.'

There's a rumour that I might be needed. There's no mention of it on the call-sheet so it seems a distinct possibility. The head boy has sent an emissary to check that I'm made-up, and I get my orders to make down the cliff on to the beach where my first scene will be shot.

I scramble down the cliff like a Women's Institute

rambler rather than a superfit mercenary. I'm saying the lines over to myself as I go: 'Four minutes and sixteen seconds, then they rendezvous with the yacht and we are back in Martinique before dawn.'

I needn't have rushed. They've got to get the camera and the lights on to the beach, and they all have to be carried at shoulder level like coffins.

The advice is going through my mind: Oliver Reed and his whispering giant, Malcolm and his 'believe in the power to be evil' and Billy Connolly, 'the first time will be the most embarrassing.'

I meet the lady with whom I shall play this scene. I take comfort from the delays, but sense a moment has come when it can be put off no longer. I wish I knew whose side they were all on. The costume designer has supervised the spraying of false sweat under my armpits. The guy with the hair-clippers has come down to watch, and there are about sixty other spectators; it's drawing them like a crowd to the bull ring.

We are placed on rocks with our feet on slippery pieces of rock and told quite sternly by the cameraman not to move. The sound man wants some level. That means he wants to hear the full force of my voice and adjust accordingly.

My first word is '*Schnell!*' (German for 'quick!'). I am supposed to bark this at the cliff-face down which my mercenaries are scrambling, except that there aren't any for me to look at.

A deep breath.

'*Schnell!*' I half bark, like a labrador letting you know it's there rather than trying to scare you off. Then I click my stopwatch as instructed and turn to the lady. My eyes are wedged open and staring, just like Ollie advised. There's going to be nothing Bambi-like about Kessler.

'Four minuts unt zixteen zekonts . . . zen ze rendezvous wiz zer yot, unt ve are bek in Martinique before dorn.'

'Great,' shouts Dick. 'We can't hear you for the waves on the beach, can you give it a bit more voice?'

(Ollie had said, 'Look the sound man in the eye and tell

him you've come three thousand miles to play this part so he'd better get it!' I decide instead to speak up.)

'Turn the camera,' screams the head boy into his pride and joy, his megaphone.

'Mark it,' shouts the sound man, and a lad runs in with a clapperboard and a piece of chalk between his teeth.

'Hold it!' shouts the cameraman. 'Sun's gone.' It had. Caribbean warmth had once again become Devon gloom. That little viewfinder the head boy carries is quickly pressed into service to scan the sky for a break in the cloud.

'Let's have lots of lovely hush, just like we always do when I'm in charge!' and he calls for the camera to run again.

'Mark it.'

The arms of the clapperboard smash together. I'm on.

'Action,' shouts Dick.

I'm giving this everything. The first time is the most embarrassing, so let's get it over.

'*Schnell!*' I bawl with such a force that I can hear it echo off a cliff-face a mile away. I click the stopwatch and fling my head in the woman's direction. I hate her, loathe her, despise her, am restraining myself from doing her physical damage . . . I try it half way between a whisper and a shout.

'Four minuts unt zixteen zeconts. Zen zey rendezvous wiz zer yart, unt ve are bek in Martinique before dorn.'

'Cut,' shouts Dick. I'm sweating. It's wiped off and replaced by artificial sweat – more life-like.

But I'm breathing easier. It's like the first dive or the first freefall parachute jump. Not perfect, but at least it's over.

'We'll try one more, but that was a good one, Paul,' says a relieved-looking director. I think he meant it.

Take two is easier, but the camera rocks.

Take three is easier still, but there's a shadow.

Take four is like falling off a log, except that I slither off the rock. Most unsoldierlike.

'We'll just try one more. The tide's coming in. We've got to get it this time.'

We got it. I've had my second blooding. The first was the hair, the second was the cameras. I'm in the movies, and, what's more, hardly anyone tells me how good or bad it was. I await the verdict with interest. In the meantime, thank you, Billy Connolly. It is awfully embarrassing, but only for a couple of minutes and who can't live with that?

The reaction comes next morning. It takes me a bit by surprise.

'I've heard about you, you're the geezer from the BBC. I heard you did well yesterday. I'm going to have to watch it.' He spits a bit of cigar end from his mouth and stomps down to the cottage to make-up. He's first on the set as usual, on location before any of us, ready and made-up while we are still like wasps round the marmalade jar, and with an instinctive sense of what the day might hold before a thought has crossed anybody else's mind. It's Michael Caine. We could be acting together today.

It's a bit like bumping into the Queen in the bus queue. I've got used to Billy Connolly's early morning jest, but Caine is a star of such magnitude that it requires no effort on his part to make his presence felt. No jokes, no gagging with the boys. He's out of the chauffeur-driven Mercedes, and it is as if some magnet has been energised. All around him are drawn to mental attention. If he asks questions, he won't expect silly answers. If he's not happy it will only take him one sharp word to have it rectified. If he's got a suggestion to make, only fools ignore it. He has authority without being an ogre and everybody loves him for it. And this man said *I* was good! It was no bullshit; he wouldn't waste his time trying to butter me up.

On a new wave of confidence I head for the costume wagon and for make-up. My senses have been dulled a little by this unexpected compliment, to the point where I fail to detect Connolly coming towards me and neglect to take swift avoiding action. He's in costume too, with his beret, guns and khaki uniform.

'Ha ha! We were talking about you last night, laddie.

Ha ha! Not bad, eh?' I took that to be a compliment too.
Having a one-hour session ahead of you for the placing of
the scar is always a good excuse for moving on, so I do.

Caine's senses are working well today. No one knows
how he does it, but even if he is asleep in his dressing-
room he will know precisely what is happening on the set.
He'll sense the problems and, without obviously inter-
fering, he'll make suggestions. He seems to know half an
hour before anybody else when he'll be needed, and
mentally prepares himself with the help of another cigar.
Perhaps the power lies in the throne – the canvas folding
chair with MICHAEL CAINE in black letters along the back-
rest. There's a pile of these chairs round the back of the
cottage and it crosses my mind to have a look to see if my
. . . but no, Ollie told me that three-liners get put in the
field with the cattle.

Caine knows he's powerful and can destroy any actor
who might cross him, so, like the nation with the ultimate
weapon, he never uses it. Quite the reverse. He'll appear
on the set and in an absent-minded way enquire, 'What's
the bunny on this one . . . ?' (slang for 'what are the
words?').

He doesn't need to ask, he knows; but everyone is put at
their ease. On the set he's called Sir. No snide intent
either.

So here I sit on a stool at the feet of this cigar-chewing
giant, cross-legged and smoking a cigar.

'It's no big deal doing a scene with me. You've been to
RADA, haven't you? Well that's the worst bit over,' and
he chuckles. 'I always work in a very relaxed way on the
set and I hope that will be catching. What you've got to
remember is that movie acting is not acting. It's reacting.
And *don't blink*.'

(I've heard this somewhere before.)

'Don't blink, because on the screen your eyes are ten
feet across and if you blink it makes you look weak. You
think about it. If someone's telling you an interesting story,
you don't sit there blinking. You listen to what they're
saying.'

I remind him that I'm playing Kessler and we have a fight scene together. He knows already.

'Just be tough. Don't try and look tough. A lot of people come on the screen and try and look like a tough guy, but that doesn't work. Don't react to people quickly, show no warmth, eyes cold, don't smile and you'll be all right. You'll be amazed how easy it is. You really will.' He leans over to me, 'I'll foul up the first take so you won't feel so bad.'

Caine senses something is happening on the set which might need his attention. God knows how he knows, but he knows. As he gets up, he reminds me, 'Don't act. That's the biggest mistake you could make. If you start giving a performance, the camera will spot it straight away. So *don't act.*'

And he's off down the hill.

'What are we doing?' I hear him ask in the distance, knowing full well *exactly* what's going on. But it's nothing involving me.

I now have three long days in which to digest Caine's concise advice. I've been on this Devon hillside a week now and I've done about a dozen words. And that's more than some of the others can say.

A short command from the head boy, and I realise that my time has come. Caine's there already, as usual; high on the oil rig, chatting with the fight-arranger and Dick Clement.

'He could run up here, place the bombs, dart round the back, fire the trigger mechanism, dash round here, fire twice and then get hold of . . .' improvises the stunt man, seeing this as a climax to a Bond film.

Clement sees it differently.

'We'll keep it simple. Paul,' and he looks around for me, 'you run up the iron stairs, creep along while Michael is looking up and take him by surprise. Get him round the throat and do the lines.'

Hell! The lines! What are they? I dredge them up from

the bottom of my mind, where they have settled and become submerged by the week's inactivity.

CAINE: Who are you, why are you here?
ME: For the bloodshed and the money. We are the dogs of war!
CAINE: Who's paying you? It's the French, isn't it. I can smell the garlic on your breath.

I then deliver Caine a punch to the gut and flee.

The stunt-arranger is called Bill Weston. He looks more like a movie hero than any of us. Well spoken in a public-school sort of way, lean, blond, could well have been an SAS man. I'd enquired about his background the other day.

'Sort of military,' was the most I could discover.

'You're not walking like a soldier. Keep your back straight and move with your legs and feet. Keep that hand on the trigger of your gun, the other hand underneath, and look as though you're ready to fire at any moment.'

This was useful advice for someone who had been holding his rifle like a rolled umbrella.

'Just do the running-up-the-stairs bit,' says Caine, help-fully. 'Then there'll be another shot where you get me round the neck.'

Cameras are ready to turn. I am at the bottom of an iron staircase and waiting for my cue. There doesn't seem much point in looking mean at this stage – I'm basically a shadowy figure in the distance – but I try it just the same.

The headboy shouts '*Stand by!*' through his megaphone. I look at Caine and wind myself up to the point where I could happily kill him, pump every bullet in this rifle into his body. I can feel my pulse quickening, I'm starting to tremble, the breathing is becoming shallower; I'll be pant-ing by the time I reach him. This is now real rage, I'll be uncontrollable by the time I get there.

'*Action!*'

With the first footstep, I swear blind to myself that I'll kill him. I charge forward and reach the point where my hands close around his throat.

'Cut!'

'Great,' shouts Dick and they set up for the next shot – me and Caine together.

'What you've got to do, Paul, is make sure all the time that you can see the lens of the camera, and then you know you're in the picture. If you can't see it, then try and feel it,' suggests Caine, more generous than most actors, who would quite happily have seen me disappear into the shadows.

The camera is in its new position.

'*Action.*'

Caine does his line first. He's looking upwards to deliver it so can't see my approach from underneath. I spring up, wrap my fingers around his throat and look as though I am squeezing the life out of him. No acting, just as Caine ordered. I have it in my mind to finish him off. Anger and rage is boiling up from the very depth of me. I look him straight in the eye, unblinking and deliver the lines. It comes out in German although I'm not trying. This is not acting, this is *being* evil. When they shout 'cut!' my head is spinning, I can hardly stop panting.

Caine leans over when the others are out of earshot, 'That was pretty good, I didn't even have to cock it up for you.'

Like Connolly said, the second time is easier, the third time it's a doddle.

'Very, very good,' says Clement.

'That's 'cos you've got two pros working up here,' says Caine. I visibly swell with pride.

'I want to try one more,' says Clement, 'with your faces a bit closer together.'

I move my lips to within inches of Caine's.

'Any closer and it will be your first screen kiss,' says Clement, and the whole crew double up with laughter.

Now for the punch to the gut.

'Have you done this before?' asks Caine, concerned.

'No,' I reply.

'Oh, bloody hell!' says Caine. 'For God's sake don't get too carried away.'

Bill Weston, the stunt arranger, reappears and tells me to fling my fist at his gut and just stop short.

'Bend your fist upwards just as you meet his body and you'll be OK.'

I try it. It has the force of a drunk sliding a billiard cue. It needs power behind it.

The camera is reset.

'*Action!*'

We do the lines again and I tense myself to fling a punch at Caine's stomach. I wind myself up to fever pitch again, and concentrate so hard on delivering this blow that I miss the cue and wind Caine halfway through his lines. It takes the merry crew some time to recover from that one too.

And then it's all over. Thirty seconds on screen, three hours to film. I'm lonely again. The cameras, the lights and the crew are moving on to the next shot and I'm left standing. The party is over. What had started out as a dread has become a treat. I want more of this elixir. This is heady stuff, movie-acting. Caine comes over.

'You did good, soldier, you really did. There's a bug in there somewhere, isn't there? You've enjoyed all this a bit too much. You'll get home and be doing your job and you'll say to yourself, "Jesus, it was good doing that one, and you'll hand in your resignation . . . and be out of work for five years." He laughs, and is away to the next shot.

I climb the hill for the last time and sit down in the cottage. No offers to wash my socks this time. It has all been going on so long that I swear my hair is beginning to grow again. I feel the pain of the removal of the scar for the last time, get out of my combat jacket and boots and slip back into slacks and beige sweater. How stupid the haircut looks without a machine gun and artificial sweat.

And when I leave this acre of unreality, set apart from the real world, and people ask me what I did to my hair, will they really believe it when I tell them, 'Oh, I was in this movie, with Michael Caine'?

I'm not certain that even I can believe it as I sit in this cinema. What if they've cut me out, what if Kessler's best lines have hit the cutting-room floor? I'm prepared for that.

All those adverts for drinks on a stick have never seemed so long. Then a tedious short about some bicycle race in East Africa, then another interval, and we're on. At least, I might be.

As the film starts, I'm desperately trying to remember the story. Where does Kessler come in it? Have they passed my bit yet? Have I been cut out or is my scene still to come?

Suddenly this figure appears on the screen. He fills it. Eyes ten feet across, just like Caine said. I am prepared to believe it was someone else. The powerful stride, the unblinking, killer stare of the soldier is there. No doubt about his nationality, no doubt that he holds that gun in the manner of a man who has killed and would do so again. He takes hold of Caine's throat with a power that worries Caine, you can read it in his eyes. And then it's all gone. I'm panting again, short of breath, sweating.

The credits roll. Caine, Connolly, Rossiter, Vaccaro, McKay . . . and then at the very end:

KESSLER .... Paul Heiney

But I'm the only one left in the cinema to see it.

Afterword
by Libby Purves (Mrs Paul Heiney)

Most women only marry one man at a time. The principle is *caveat emptor* – if you marry an athlete, you put up with his training schedule, and if you tie yourself to a farmer you accept the prospect of mud on the kitchen floor. I have had to get used to a succession of different husbands within four years, and very confusing it has been too.

When I met Paul, he was a good-tempered radio and television reporter, with the usual amused detachment of a working journalist. He, and I, were happy to believe that actors are unreasonably neurotic, and horsey people boring; that shepherds just sit on hills, hairdressers are limp-wristed poseurs, *haute cuisine* a bit of a con-trick, and that if we happened to feel like it we could do a better job any day than the feeble stand-up comics on TV. We may not have voiced these opinions, but to some extent we both had them. This book has been an account of how we both learned humility: Paul at first-hand, I at second. If he was up in the front line, dicing carrots and herding sheep, I was sweating too, back at GHQ, and I never knew what sort of man I would get back at the end of each filming trip. So, bravely, Paul has invited me to add a few domestic observations to his story. Here they are.

The first time I realised how deep beneath his skin these enterprises were getting was when he came home from his first visit to Swingletree Stables. The black cat jumped on his knee, and he stared at it thoughtfully. He had not said much since he got in, but suddenly:

'Cats,' he said. 'Cats. Very small, aren't they?' I waited, not quite knowing how to follow this one up. 'Very small. After horses.' And he pushed the surprised animal off his knee, and started threading the curtain-drawstrings through his fingers, frowning. I did not realise at the time that they had just turned into leather reins.

In a few weeks, the effort of learning to drive had utterly taken over. Bits of dungy straw fell from his pockets. He took to mooching round London saddlers and country gents outfitters, criticising the seams on the driving-gloves. He took me down, too, to Swingletree Stables, and John Parker fixed me with the famous gimlet eye, noting my tremulous first pregnancy, and warned me that Paul would have to be away from home, training, 'a lot'. Luckily, I fell equally in love with the horses and with John and Susan, and spent the summer lumbering around bumpy marathon courses watching them all work. The final moment of commitment came in the caravan on that terrible day at Windsor after Agy nearly died. I knew then that if Paul was negligent on his big day, and hurt one hair of one of those horses, I too would find it difficult to forgive him. When it came to the water obstacle at Wramplingham, Susan ran away and wouldn't watch; and I stood by the river-bank, seven months gone, with tears of relief and delight running down my face.

It was not so, alas, with the dog. Poor old Tim. The producer of the programme had said to me over a drink too many at Christmas that the sheepdog 'might have to spend six weeks or so living with Paul, to create a bond'. No problem, I said generously. In the end, it was five months, and a fearful problem. Tim's hobby, as Paul has mentioned, was barking; starting at 5 am, it invariably woke the baby for the day. Tim also comprehensively ruined our family walks. The trouble with dog-handlers is that they become horribly authoritarian, I could almost say fascist – indeed, I did say so, often. It was like having a walk with Mussolini: Tim could not be allowed one moment of independent snuffling or loping around, without a roar of *'Stand there!'* or *'That'll do!'* from the Great Dictator at my side. The baby loved it – used to roar 'Dat'll do!' at his teddy every night – but occasionally the Tim-discipline habit spilt over into domestic discussions, very perilous. Much as I grew to respect the skills and the character of

Norman Seamark, I regret to tell you that at that famously affecting moment on the film when the dog was finally handed back, I was dancing a jig of unrestrained glee just off-camera. It was amazing how quickly I got my mild, unauthoritarian, pleasantly wimpish husband back again.

Not for long, alas. Before many months had gone by he was wandering around the garden threatening the hollyhocks. 'I tolt you olt man to leef her allone . . . Schweinhund!' he would shout. The neighbour would raise his old head from his broad beans and stare in simple wonder. 'Hah! For zer blutshed and zer money!' cried the aspiring actor. Then he would pop back into the kitchen and absentmindedly call me sweetie, and wonder about his costume. After a week or two on location in Devon for *Water*, phoning most irritatingly 'from the poolside radiophone' (it rained all summer in Suffolk), he returned, and his appalling John McVicar haircut nearly brought on the next baby a month early.

I am, on the whole, glad I didn't marry an actor, but even gladder not to be shackled to a failed comedian. Never shall I forget the night when, at 1 am, a shattered remnant of a man crept into bed, having died his first death at an unforgiving dive called the Comedy Store. Nor the final débâcle at the Lakeside Club when, having become roaring drunk out of sheer nerves, I watched his act and its reception in silent horror and then lunged across the table to grab the nervously giggling head of his BBC department by the satin DJ-lapels. 'You bashtard,' I slurred, 'you owe him a contract for life, for this!'

Compared to that, the rest was plain sailing. I fear I was little help in the composition of the romantic story for *Woman's Weekly*, although we used to walk along the beach trying to improvise affecting dialogue for his current boring hero and heroine. It usually went:

'You – you do care, don't you? Care, I mean? about – well, people?'

'One person – but you don't want to know that, do you? Damn you!'

'Oh Sam, I – I – don't know what to say. Except . . . goodbye,' and so on, for as long as we could stand it.

I am constantly told how lucky I am to have such a 'useful' husband with all these wonderful skills – especially cooking and hairdressing. Alas, although he was at one point such a dedicated hairdresser that when introduced to a new woman he would gaze straight into her fringe, not bothering with the face at all, the urge soon faded after the big day, and my hair was dismissed out of hand all along as 'not the sort he'd practised on'. As for cooking, what you have to understand about trainee chefs is that they are so wrapped up in the pursuit of perfection that they become unable, after a few sessions with M. Roux, to knock up a herb omelette or steam a piece of broccoli without putting on a freshly starched white jacket and a tall hat, getting out a suitcaseful of assassin's knives, and dirtying every pan and dish in the kitchen. The omelette, on the other hand, is perfect.

So what remains of all this effort, apart from a few photographs and some rather dubious baggy trousers (as worn by Leading Stylists) in which he occasionally creates a sensation at Saxmundham market? Well, two shaggy black fell-ponies, to start with: Ebony and China, who were the closest, cheapest thing we could get to Agy and Bollio's white splendour. We bowl around the lanes, doing obstacle-drives round old treetrunks, and dream of past glory. John Parker is our eldest child's godfather and one day promises he will teach him to drive as he taught his father. There is a deep and abiding fear of cabarets and nightclubs (when Paul sees a shaded electric candle he goes rigid), and an enviable ability to cut our children's hair himself (our son is stoically resigned to being called Madam in absent moments). There is the occasional superb omelette, and a rusting old dog-chain in the orchard. But above all, there is a legacy of respect for the real professionals: the too-often unsung heroes and heroines who really can control horses, dogs, sauces, audiences, and hair. And for their long-suffering spouses.